To

Sri Neelakanta Pillai Swamikal

of

Suchindram

SELECTED WORKS OF SRI CHATTAMBI SWAMIKAL

TRANSLATION

S JAGATHSIMHAN NAIR

Contents

SELECTED WORKS
of
SRI CHATTAMBI SWAMIKAL

Translation by
S.Jagathsimhan Nair

Sri Vidyadhiraja Chattambi Swamikal

Acknowledgements

I gratefully acknowledge the help rendered by the retired Professor of Sanskrit, Dr. Maheswaran Nair, Thiruvananthapuram, who had compiled and edited Swamiji's works and which I have taken as the source text for translation, in clarifying certain doubts that arose during the process.

Preface

I set out on this project, on impulse. Only to find the source text to be quite unforgiving in its tenacity not to yield in its diction and content. Just when the narration looked like letting up, it doubled-down with a vengeance, leaving me lost and wondering whether to press on or quit. For one thing, it was penned in a century old version of a language, though one I was born to, nevertheless, a bit bothersome on that score; and especially with all that Sanskrit thrown in. I thought, rather unjustifiably, that though my Sanskrit was not exactly passable, I could at least make a stretch of it, to begin with, with the help of all those extensive foot notes available. But, often I found the going way too challenging . But, then, it was like a language like Sanskrit with such a high level of inflection and a none-too-easy morphology, leaving me often wishing, in vain, there was someone to help me out. To add to the challenge, it often appeared as though errors have crept into the original text, with clauses not connecting , and sentences either not making sense or looking broken, out of place or repetitive. Errors like this are likely with the reprints it might have gone through in the course of about a century of its existence when printing was totally manual. Add to it the well known hassles of translation. I had no way except skirting around certain uncompromising lines or even paragraphs while making sure not to miss the overall focus of the narrative. While in large parts, the narration is line by line, in certain others it would be abridged. What is more, certain portions , considered inconsequential or too difficult , were even excised, with the result, I am afraid, that the translation would not deserve an adjective more glorifying than ' liberal'.

Importance or lack of it.

I have chosen here only four of Sri Chatambi Swamiji's works for rendering into English. The choice did not follow any considered decision. It was rather what I thought to be the easier ones-to-translate that made the list. But once I started, accidentally with 'Ancient Malayalam' and 'Right to the Veda', I was just wondering what the heck I was up to. Before asking what, I needed to ask how, who and why . And, how does it matter today and , in fact, who cares, which caste is superior to which or who were denied the Veda and who were not and what relevance it all holds to our times. I, even as a mere translator, was , in fact, rather feeling bad as if I was myself raking up uncomfortable questions of caste and discrimination that belonged to an all-but-forgotten era and which are best left untouched. But my real reason was much simpler. I am a lazy reader, unable to focuss on what I read when it comes to works like what I have on hand. Translating was my way of overcoming the handicap, because once you are on, you need to go line by line and imbibe their meanings.Then I also took solace in the thought that may be it's my karma to do them in English in 2017, however sloppy it might appear to be, after nearly a century of its existence, almost in obscurity and oblivion even in its own land, not to speak of shores beyond. Because, the contents of these two works, however unsavoury they might appear to be, are nevertheless an account of at least a part of our recent history. But my guilt and doubts did not abate till the very end, though it was overshadowed by a new freshness that I perceived as I waded into the other two works which , while dealing with nothing as muddled as the first two, were in fact gripping for their humane content, far-sighted vision and relevance to the times. But, undoubtedly, the first two stood out for their historical significance, revolutionary fervor and lessons for the future, if any, at least for whoever that choose to look that far into the distance.

The only source material I went by was the compilation of Swamiji's works in Malayalam with notes and a biographical introduction by Dr. K. Maheswaran Nair and I record here my gratitude to him. This compilation with a content largely spiritual in nature enjoys the rare and unique distinction of having been launched by the great Sh. E.M.S. Namboodiripad, one of the finest Marxists India had ever seen, and the one who headed, as the Chief Minister of Kerala state, the first ever communist government that came to power through the ballot. Practically no independent research from this translator's side had gone into the material being dealt with. No other publication on Swamiji or his works, either old or new, had been referred to, either. About dates, names, incidents, historical references, material quoted from other works etc, I have strictly gone by what was available in the source text, without going into their correctness or absence of it. And, as such, suggestions or corrections from readers in the know of things would be most welcome.

A note on the author:

Sri Chatambi Swamikal (1853-1924) was a Hindu sage and social reformer who lived in Kerala, the state that lies to the south-west of India. Born to a Brahmin father and a Nair mother, in today's Thiruvanantapuram, his childhood was one of suffering and privation due to the straitened circumstances of his family. He initially learnt letters of the alphabet from other children, Sanskrit by overhearing classes and something more formal under a kindly Raman Pilla Asan who taught him for free. He also benefited from the discussions at the meetings of learned men, Raman Pilla Asan held regularly, until one Tamil scholar, one Subba Jatapatikal, took Chattambi along to his place, Kalladakurichi, in Tamil Nadu where he lived for some years , far away from home, presumably learning things that needed to be learnt those days. After his return, he unexpectedly runs into an ascetic at the present-day Nagercoil, and receives from him Diksha and the most sacred Bala Subrahmanya mantra by way of initiation into a deeply spiritual life. Within years, he grows into a towering personality known all over Kerala as an erudite scholar and as one capable of mind-boggling miracles, so knowledgeable and self-confident as to clarify the doubts of even personalities as redoubtable as Swami Vivekananda . Among his well known disciples are Neelakanta Teertapada and Teertapada Paramahamsa. It is said that at least according to the early biographers, Sri Chattambi Swamikal mentored the then Nanu Asan , by bestowing on him the secret and potent Bala Subramanya mantra, which, according to people in the know, is 'Mantra diksha', the ultimate act of help a master can do to his disciple. Nanu Asan later rose to be a celebrated personality in his own right, both as a great spiritual leader and as a relentless social reformer, known all over Kerala and beyond as Sri Narayana Guru.

Chattambi Swamikal is regarded as one of the earliest crusaders against social inequality in Kerala, an area known for one of the harshest and most rigorous systems of caste that existed anywhere, at that time. It was just not the four caste system we tend to be reminded of in this context, but numerous sub castes within a broad rubric with their uncompromising segregations and divisions and taboos that culminated in the utter social exclusion and economic deprivation of some and that socially manifested in the form of the most reprehensible practice of untouchability. It was a graded social structure in which even those who belonged to an upper caste suffered terrible discrimination from a caste occupying a place just a rung above, in the social order. It was by and large Brahmins, with the exception of some Nairs, who occupied the highest rung in the social ladder who had all the wealth and exercised all the power. Some of Sri Chattambi swami's works were a direct attack on this kind of Brahmin dominance. It must have taken not a little courage on his part to have struck such a defiant posture against an authority who held the power to kill at will. His razor-sharp arguments tore apart their pet theories and exposed the hollowness of their positions. His spit-fire prose lambasted them. His words surely amped up a generation at the possibility of phenomenal social change. An iconoclast of sorts , he was often didactic to a fault too.

What follows is a note on each of these works.

1.A critique on the right to The Veda.

The quartet of Vedas or simply The Veda is considered to form the most basic and sacred document of Hinduism. During the author's time, it was not accessible in toto to anyone except the Brahmins. All the others were either barred from touching it, or listening to it or learning it. It was in such a scenario that this author mounted his challenge against this tradition and argued that everyone without distinctions should be eligible to read and learn the Veda. By challenging their most jealously and preciously guarded privilege, the swami was in effect challenging all the rest of the privileges that they were enjoying.

But this work stands out for another reason. Obviously names and reputation seemed to have mattered not a bit with this rebel-sage. It looks like he enjoyed trashing at least parts of that most sacrosanct of all documents, the Veda. It is baffling how a noted spiritual leader as the swamiji himself could pick holes at a document that was supposed to be his sacred cow, by pointing out its internal contradictions, at a time when it was unpardonable blasphemy to do so. It is interesting as well as riveting to find him chiding such a titanic figure like Sri Sankara and slagging off some of the revered commentators of Hindu theology.

2. The place of woman and man in the world

This is a very small work, based on one of his talks, but is seminal in that its emphasis on the importance of women in society caught on, to remain in the spotlight ever after. In those rather dark ages it was amazing how swamiji possessed such far-sightedness and wisdom as would fit the modern world. He establishes with lucid reasoning that woman should get more importance than man in the social order. In the modern society which still remains patriarchal and where women get more and more traumatized day by day all over the world in various ways, this could be an invaluable document of guidance for all. It would not be an overrating of it if I say that this work deserves to be made compulsory material for study in schools. Though Swamiji's narrative was based on a typical Kerala household of those days, its message essentially is universal.

3.Compassion for other living beings

This is again a topic that remains relevant for all times. Here, the swamiji is rooting for undiluted non-violence to be practiced by all. It is captivating how he takes the reader step-by-step into the pleasant discovery that it is just the practice of one hundred percent non-violence and the attitude of compassion that accompanies it that ultimately leads one to self-realization , the highest goal of human existence. It deserves to be read by one and all including school and college-going children.

4. Ancient Kerala.

This is only the first of a series of volumes Swamiji intended to write on the subject, out of which it is believed six were completed, though one alone is available in the public domain. For a people who are historically and particularly unmindful of their own histories like the Indians, the author's foray into Kerala's ancient history was not only a pleasant departure but was also by way of setting an example to his fellowmen on the importance of preserving one's own records of history. This is a well researched work that went on to prove how Brahmins who arrived from outside usurped by fair and foul means all the powers and wealth of the natives and came to dominate the society in unfair and often unkind ways. It lays bare how Mahabharat defines castes, not once but on several occasions, and how it is being practiced in violation of such guidelines. The work is not only historical but more importantly social in the sense that it turned out to be a severe indictment of the caste system that existed those days.

A Note on Transliteration

An attempt is made to avoid diacritic marks. Most words belonging to Malayalam, Sanskrit and Tamil appear in their phonetic approximations. However, in the case of popular names of persons, places, books etc, the spellings in vogue are adopted. Phonemes, naturally, become a bit confusing to pronounce. A guide to pronunciation is given below. The word-examples shown below are based on the Indian way of pronouncing them, though it is likely that some of them, though not all, would be pronounced slightly differently elsewhere.

a – as in *China.* ri – as in *river*

aa – as *a* in *far.* e – as *ay* in *say*

i – as in *pin* ai – as *i* in *rite*

ee – as in *feel* o – as in *go*

u – as in *put* au /ou – as *au* in *loud*

oo – as *u* in *rule*

k – as in *kite,* kh – as in *khan,* g – as in *gun,* gh – as in *ghost* ,

ch – as in *church,* t – as in *thallium,* tt/**t** – as *t* in *ton*

d – as *th* in *them,* dh – as in *dharma,* dd/**d** – as in *day*

ph – as in *pharmacy,* bh – as in *bharat, bhagavan,* y – as in *yes.*

s – as in *sun,* sh – as in *share,* ng – as in *sing,* nj – as *ng* in *range*

jna – pronounced rather as *jya* which is close but not quite so.

r – as in *brave* , **r** - as in *trick*

l – as in *line,* **l** - as in *blow*

n – as in *name,* **n** -as in *hundred,* <u>n</u> - as in *anthem, bandh*

CHAPTER ONE

A Critique on the Right to the Vedas. (Vedaadhikaara Niroopanam)

THE REALITY OF VEDA

There can be little doubt that the works that are of great import and moment to most people are the Vedas. People in general can be broadly classified into two, viz. theists and atheists. Atheists are not many in number. Even among them, there would be no one who believes in atheism from deep inside his heart. Theists believe in the existence of a supreme power called God. There are a whole lot of such believers around. But they belong to different groups depending upon their belief systems pertaining to matters like the concept of God, the connection between God and the universe, and God's attributes and powers.

From among these groups we need to discuss here only two viz. *SROUTAS* and *PRAPANCHA VAADIS*. Those who believe that God himself had given us the Vedas in order that we may learn about what is right/good and what is wrong/evil are the *Sroutas*. On the other hand, those who believe that God is the only protector of his creation namely the universe and universe itself is the equivalent of the Veda are the *Prapancha vaadis*. In this discussion it would not be out of place to take into account the views of the above mentioned groups also.

What is Veda? Who is its author? How many of them are there? These are some of the questions being asked in this connection. Some say it has no author, some say it is the record of sayings of sages and some others opine that it was created by God himself. A few think it is countless, most regard it as the most important of all ancient literature and some believe that it was written by human beings. Although it occupies a pride of place among knowledge systems handed down to us by oral traditions and since at least a few believe that Veda loses some of its importance when subjected to evidence-based scrutiny, we need to critique each one of these views separately.

What does the word Veda mean is what we are going to look at first. In order to get a comprehensive understanding of the meaning of a word, we need to correlate the meanings and purposes of its equivalent words. Therefore, to get a proper sense of the word, Veda, one has to look for it along with its synonyms.

The author of '*Amarakosham*' says that the three words, Veda, *Sruti* and *Amnaaya* have the same meaning. Veda by one definition is that with the help of which one is able to discern what is righteous and what is not. The second definition says that something that creates awareness is Veda. But both the definitions carry the same meaning although the way they are spelt out are different. Further, according to '*Shabda ratnaavali*', the word '*Brahmam-Nigamam*' and according to *Jataadhara*, the word

'*Pravachanam*[1]' are the synonyms of the word 'Veda'. Normally, brahma gnani or the one who has realized the Ultimate Truth is considered to be the one who has also realized that he and *Brahman*(the Supreme Cosmic Power) are one and the same. But to the exclusion of such a grand meaning, if a person who had just about learnt what was *Brahman* from his masters came to be described as *Brahmin* meaning one who had experienced the state of *Brahman*, it might be merely due to the presence of the brahma-word in the above context than anything more substantial than that.

The works going by the name of Veda throw light on the nature and attributes of the individual and universal souls. But the universe too does the same thing in its own way. Because of this, the *Prapanchavaadis*claim that the word Veda should not only be considered as referring to those books, but should also be treated as a synonym for universe itself.

Now, let us see about the word '*Sruti*'. One view is that Veda came to be called *Sruti* because it is from Veda that one gets to hear about *Dharma* (righteousness) and *Adharma*, the opposite of *Dharma*. The other view about it is much simpler, viz. 'that which one gets to hear is *Sruti*'. *Sroutas* maintain that it is called *Sruti* because it is heard directly from God. But, *Prapanchavadis*hold a different view. It is like this. Since most of the works now named Veda came into being at a time when letters of alphabets have not evolved and its message got transmitted from one person to another by word of mouth, it came to be called by the name '*Pravachanam*' which literally means prediction. Another synonym of veda agrees with this view of the Prapancha vaadis. *Aamnaya* is that which gets handed down through generations. It came to be called

'Aamnaya' because its words were handed down from father to son and from son to grand son etc. These views differ from each other. We, therefore, need to examine whether it was created at all by man or by some superior power.

Sroutas do not consider it as created by man. For them it is god's own creation. Their main arguments are as follows.

1.Whatever is said in the Veda is found to be true. Further, a dictum of Veda itself is that gods alone are true and humans are not. So Veda has got to be Gods' own creation.

2.*Smrutis* state categorically that there are no authors as such for the Veda.

3.Even in this age of advanced knowledge and civilization, Veda is revered. It is therefore improbable that it was created by men of the dark ages.

4.In order to make people pious and righteous, there is need for a work of divine nature with moral and ethical content. Veda serves this purpose well. Naturally, it should be of divine origin.

5.The epics and *Puranas*[2] were created by great sages. But Veda is recognized as ranking in stature above such works from very early times. So, it follows that it is impossible for man to have created the Veda.

But *Prapanchavaadis*counter these views with the following argument.

1.It is not correct to claim that Veda is always true or infallible. Just try to take a look at its rhetorical and explanatory content. Most of it belongs to *Karma kanda* (domain of action) and a little of it to *Brahma kanda* (domain of true knowledge). It is widely accepted that many of the things contained in the *Karma* kanda have to be rejected. For example, can anyone justify by any means the animal sacrifice being practised during *Yajnas* or Sacrificial fires.

'The Veda deals with what is not obvious and, as such, it imparts knowledge to the uninitiated'

Just like bitter pills are given a coating of sugar, Veda propounds the theory of action (*karma*) only as a means to achieving liberation from action . But, according to *Srimad* Bhaagavatam, people without understanding this secret message, go about holding *Yajnas* or sacrificial ceremonies involving sacrificing of animals, which in time inexorably return to haunt and destroy the masters of such ceremonies themselves.

Swami *Brahmananda Saraswati*[3] deplores this slaughter of animal life thus.

'It is clearly said in the Veda that no living being should be killed. Trivialising such a strict stipulation, the evil priests argue in favour of animal sacrifice in rituals where Fire and '*Soma*' spirit are supposed to be the premier presiding gods. That such slaughter like any other slaughter is equally violent and unjustifiable is the view in Sri *Bhoja*'s commentary on the '*Yoga Sutra*'of *Patanjali*.

Further, to quote what transpires between Lord *Shiva* and Goddess *Parvati* as contained in *Padma purana*:

'Those who slaughter creatures either in the name of *Shakti* worship or for other ceremonial purposes will have no escape from the horrors of the hell called *Kumbhipakam*[4]. Those who kill in the name of general sacrifices or as obsequies/ libations to departed souls or as a means of livelihood will have to rot in the hell named *Rauravam*[5]. If Heaven's doors are going to be opened to those who tie up the sacrificial animal in the designated stake at first and then proceed to kill it with its blood being spilt, one wonders what kind of action is supposed to open the doors of Hell'.

Sage *Vyasa*'s above words could not have been more bitter in decrying the practice of sacrifices.

In a sacrifice named *Poundarika Yajna*, the coitus between a widow and a *brahmachari*(celibate or one who is supposed to have no union with a woman in thought, word or deed) is permitted by the Veda.

The book *Ashwamedha prakarana* says the reigning queen has to insert the organ of a stallion (male horse)into her private part during that sacrifice.

In the *Mahavruta* sacrifice, sex between courtesan and *brahmachari*(celibate) is permitted.

But such reprehensible practices as described above will not be tolerated or supported by the pious people, even if one thousand Vedas sponsor them. Is it not the reason why some of the practices that Veda sanctions without consideration to either place or time are getting debunked by the scholars on the subject.

Brihannarayanya purana prohibits five things in the Age of *Kali* or Evil (Mankind is supposed to be living in the *Kali* age for more than five thousand years now). They are *Aswamedha*(sacrifice involving horse), *Gomedha* (sacrifice involving cow), *Sanyas* (life of renouncement of all pleasures of life), Meat eating during observance of ceremonies meant for departed souls, and Getting pregnant from the younger brother of one's husband. Such prohibitions could only mean that there are flaws and deficiencies in the Veda. Leaving it aside for a moment, it is well known that the Quran of the Muslims, the Bible of the Christians and the Veda of the Hindus are claimed to be records of the words of God. But some of their contents are found to be contrary to each other. If there are two contrary views, at least one has to be untrue. Naturally, such a view can not be considered as God-given. If the first and second among these three are untrue, how is it that the third could be true. But if the claim is that it must be true just because generations of our ancestors believed so, then, such a view is vain and irrational. In conclusion, unless and until it is decided conclusively and in unassailable terms as to what part of it is god-given and what is human-created, none of it should be considered as God-gifted.

It would be more in order to consider all of them as creations of man. It would make little difference even if it is explicitly stated in the work itself that it is god-given. One has also to ponder about the fact that some of the recent works by authors who are not *Prapanchavaadis*are far more extensive than any of these Vedas, almost every one of which is much smaller in comparison. The antique nature of these works should not make one conclude that they are of divine origin. It is not at all surprising to find a couple of scholars among a multitude of ordinary folks being looked upon by the majority as carrying some divinity in them. It is not only true in this land but even in countries like Greece, Rome and England, according to their histories. That the Vedas were born of such authors invested with divinity by common people should not make them objects of slander or ridicule. Some may argue that whatever someone in a sudden spell of trance utter must be considered as issuing forth from God himself. But it must be kept in mind that only the unlettered, the insane and the drunkard go through such spells and the others do not. And therefore such people do not merit consideration as some kind of oracles. Since intelligence and knowledge on the part of an individual are normally considered as gifted by God, some may argue that works of scholars should also be treated as divine pronouncements. If it is so, would it be possible for us to consider our own writings, endowed as we are with a certain quantum of intelligence and understanding, as the words of gods or as Veda itself.

It is true that we need to have ' something' that would enable us to discriminate between what is righteous and what is not. When God had given us this Universe itself as that 'something', it is lackadaisical on our part to go after other things. When it is almost impossible for one to study this universe all by himself and make his progress in life too, the question arises as to whether a book of divine nature by way of guidance would not be advisable to have. The answer would be Yes, if there is indeed one. In its absence, what is the use of assumin there is one. Instead of God giving us his book, it would have been really helpful if only he had, in his infinite mercy, chosen to appear before us and give us his words of wisdom. But is it in the realm of possibility? Absolutely not.

Ancient sages have told us that works like *Puranas*, Epics etc carry the core message of the Veda. We should realize that primary evidence is more important than the secondary one. Nothing is going to be God-given just because some people say so. From what has been handed to us by the thinkers of the earliest times, we should recognize the parts of it which are blemishless in nature and accept them. Something does not become ineligible for acceptance, just because it does not trace its origin to God. Accepting and adopting what is good in such works will be of use to us only.

'*Anan̲ta vai veda*' is a dictum the *Sroutas* believe in, which means the Vedas are countless. The take of *Prapanchavaadis*on this subject is that whichever work conveys through its sounds and meanings the nature of Almighty and what is righteous and what is not, deserves to be called Veda. But, to perform such a function, there is nothing better than this universe itself. But the extent and constituents of this universe are infinite and immeasurable. And hence the implication of the above dictum is that only the Veda in the form of universe is limitless, and not the Veda in the form of books.

2. VEDA'S PRE-EMINENCE

The three accepted modes of acquiring knowledge are these: 1) By direct observation 2) by inference and 3) through sounds or oral means. Doubtlessly, the Veda belongs to the sound/oral category. A comparative look at these three would help us get an idea about the reality of the Veda. To explain by means of an example: If I see , with my own eyes, Mr. Deva dutta eating , the information is first-hand or directly experienced. It is through the second mode, if I infer that he must have eaten because his belly looks full. Someone telling you that he had eaten belongs to the third type. A person's belly could appear full due to reasons other than eating, like say, indigestion. Similarly, oral information received from a third party could go wrong on two counts , namely, the info could have been misunderstood by that person in the first place or he could even be trying to misguide or fool you. Because of these reasons, if one is to make a ranking of these three modes of receiving knowledge in the order of their importance, direct experience is the best and the most reliable, the method of inference is about weak, and oral communication is the weakest and themost undependable. Though Veda enjoys premier acceptability among all our oral traditions of passing on knowledge, it is undoubtedly the weakest in terms of reliability when compared to info obtained through the direct and inference methods. That is the reason why past scholars have set aside as adulatory and deprecatory certain portions of the Veda which do not tally with experience.

To quote from The *Bhagavad Gita* and *Maandookya Upanishad*:

'OM', the single syllable, is Brahman (the Supreme Power)

All (in this world) is 'OM'.

Grammatically 'OM' means:

'That which is about Light' and 'that which is all-protecting in nature'

'OM' is Brahman in the form of sound.

Brahman is OM-manifested.

Both 'OM' and Brahman are one and the same. There is little difference between the two. That is the reason why there is no separation between the two in the *Maandookya Upanishad* etc.

But thinking rationally, one would be tempted to perceive some difference between the two, though.

But since practicing OM according to prescribed rules is found to endow the practitioner with liberation from earthly bonds, we would only look at its significance in the light of what is said in the *Upanishads*.

1.OM, the all-encompassing sound from the earliest beginnings, is indeed the Veda.

As already told, OM is Brahman itself. It therefore follows that Veda in the form of OM is without beginning and end like *Brahman.*

2.Veda recital should begin and end with chanting of OM. Failure to chant OM in the beginning will make one forget the Veda slowly. Failure to do so at the end will result in non-retention of what was learnt, in one's memory.

3. The sacrificial rituals prescribed in the Veda provide only temporary results. That is, they are ephemeral in

nature. But OM that makes one realize the Ultimate leading to one's Liberation is eternal and imperishable in its substance.

The two preceding statements should justify the earlier assertion that OM and *Brahman* are one and the same.

Here is how Brahman or God Almighty is defined in ancient texts.

'That which is obvious and , at the same, not; that which constitutes the cause and effect of everything; that which is immanent in the thirty six values, while at the same time transcending them; that which is not bound to Time, past, present and future; that which is beyond knowability, knowledge and knower, but all the same perceivable to the great Sages; that which is the source of all *mantras* starting from OM, that which is too subtle to be envisioned by the mind; that which accommodates all, while pervading all, like space; and that which infuses life into all that is dead; I meditate on such glorious face of Brahma.'

On the basis of the aforementioned reasons, one arrives at the conclusion that the Veda is not different from the OM-manifested-*Brahman*, that it is without beginning and end, that it is not the creation of mankind but of God Himself, and that it is the greatest and noblest of all else.

To quote from *Mundaka Upanishad*:

'*Rig, Yajur, Sama and Atarva* Vedas are not at all important. Nor are the Vedangas or Veda's offshoots namely *Shiksha, Kalpa, Vyakarana, Chandas, Jyotisha and Nirukta*. What is really important is that which enables one to reach the Eternal Reality of this universe. The Veda that does not help one in this regard can not be called Veda at all. Because, Veda is that by which one is able to realize that Eternal Truth. Naturally, such a sublime state of Realisation has got to be boundless, timeless and creator-less.

We ascribe certain portions of the Veda to the Sages and certain others to man. Every *mantra* in the Veda is found associated with some sage(***Rishi***) or other, a certain metrical arrangement of words (*Chandas*), and a particular deity(*Devata*). So in *sutras* or self-standing stanzas, its author (sage), its metrical arrangement and its presiding deity are found mentioned. For example, *Rig* veda's very first *mantra* has sage *Madhu*(son of sage *Viswamitra*) as its ***Rishi***, the metrical system, *Gayatri* for *Chandas* and *Agni*(Fire god) for deity. It therefore follows that the sage associated with any *mantra* is its author. If someone doubts it because it is not unambiguously stated so, let us examine this line from *Mantra prasna* (*Thaithariya aaranyaka*).

'*Namah, rishibhyo mantra kritbhya*', which means

'Salutations to the sages who created the *mantras*'.

To quote from *Srimad* Bhaagavatam:

'In the beginning, OM alone was the Veda. But later, the King *Purooravas* created three Vedas'.

So, it goes without saying that it was *Purooravas* who authored at least certain portions of the Veda.

To quote from *Vishnu puranam*:

'Sage *Vaisampaayana*, the son of sage *Vyasa*, is the creator of the twenty seven branches *Yajur veda* now has'.

To quote from *Chandogya Upanishad*, seventh chapter:

'When sage *Narada* wants to be taught by *Sanal kumara*, who enquires about the level of the seeker's former learning. Finding that *Narada* had already learnt the four Vedas, *Sanal kumara* teaches him that which is thereafter recorded in the seventh chapter of *Chandogya*'.

This shows that *Sanal kumara* had added something of his own to the four Vedas which were already in existence. This seems to have happened from time to time with the Veda, with different authors contributing at different points of time.

Sage *Brihaspati*has no difficulty accepting that veda has authors. Being angered by some of its contents, he however proceeds to snub them by calling them a bunch of good-for-nothing flatterers, prodigals and monsters.

It was earlier stated that knowledge coming through the medium of the spoken word is the least acceptable. Veda's message is one such. But this fact should in no way eclipse or belittle its *Advaitic* (non-dual) philosophy. *Advaitic* doctrine postulates that there is absolutely no difference between the individual and cosmic consciousness. In all the other philosophies which do not propound this non-dual principle, this universe is very much real. But not so, according to the *Advaitic* doctrine. According to it, the way the universe appears is as unreal as perceiving a cobra in a small length of rope lying on the ground in semi-darkness or as illusory as the images thrown up by a mirage. As such, only those religious doctrines that consider this world as real could be included within the ambit of the different philosophies that sought to prove that the world as very much real. Such a grand and elegant philosophy as the Veda, that demolished the view that the world was real with sound reasoning and supporting evidence and that remained above reproach and stood out as the proponent of the *Advaitic* (non-dual) doctrine, should not at all suffer any diminution in its worth or stature .

If, all the same, *Sroutas* continue to maintain that the world is very much real and theirs is God's own word, it must be more due to false pride than sound reasoning.

And, the work, *Vaasishtam*, justifies the harsh language of a bristling *Brihaspati* thus:

'With the passage of time there was ingress of new ideas into the Veda, depending upon the mindset and thinking of the people of the times. Untruths, violent tenets and other deplorable stuff found their way into the Veda, influenced, as they were, by evil-minded scholars who lived from time to time. *Brihaspati*'s rage is due to the fact that such unhealthy intrusions which should have been rejected then and there were regrettably found retained as part of the Veda'.

-3-

CRITIQUE OF THE RIGHT TO THE VEDA

Let us now examine the debate going on for quite some time now, on the comparative rights on the subject of learning of the Veda. There is a general belief among sections of the people that there are stipulations that insist that only *Brahmin*s are empowered to learn Veda and impart/interpret it to others, that *Kshatriyas* and *Vaishyas* can learn but not teach/interpret and that *Sudra* can neither learn nor teach/interpret. If one looks for rules in support of that belief, as far as I know, there is none which bars *Kshatriya* from imparting knowledge or *Sudra* from acquiring it. If someone happens to show that there is such a rule in existence, we will consider it at that time. On the contrary, one could cite a number of instances from the Veda itself where *Kshatriya* teaches and *sudra* learns. A few of them are given below.

In *Brihadaranyaka Upanishad* (2nd chapter, 1st braahmanam), a *Brahmin* named *Gaargya* is said to have acquired Vedic knowledge from a *kshatriya* king called *Ajaata shathru*.

Gaargya tells *Ajaata shathru*: 'I am serving you like how a true disciple should serve his master'.

To this, Ajaata replies: ' A *Brahmin* who is supposed to be a Teacher himself seeking and receiving such knowledge from a *kshatriya* is against tradition. However, I will impart the *Brahmic* knowledge to you'.

He had uttered these words only out of extreme modesty.

Chandogya narrates another story. Five sages named *Praachina shaalan* (son of *Upamanyu*), *Satyaprajna (Poulushi), Indra dyumna, Janan, and Budila,* finding themselves befuddled trying to unravel the complexities in their pursuit of the *Brahmic* Truth approaches sage *Uddaalaka* seeking help. *Uddaalaka*, in turn, takes them to King *Aswapati* and requests: ' Is it not that what you should receive is what you seek to get? What we want is the *Brahmic* knowledge of the *Vaiswaanara* kind, which you are a master of. Please instruct us on that'. The King agrees and asks them to present themselves before him next morning. They duly do as directed and acquire the Divine knowledge. In the process, the king warns them of what would have happened to them, had they continued with their incorrect practices and not approached him for directions.

'One would have lost his head, the second would have lost his life, the third, his eye sight and the fourth, his leg etc'.

This only shows how much more advanced and superior was the knowledge the *kshatriya* possessed than that of those *Brahmins*. It also affirms that *kshatriya* is qualified not only to teach, but teach *Brahmins* too.

Again, from *Chandogya*, 5th chapter:

Shwetaketu (*Brahmin*), the son of *Aaruni*, gets bested, in a Vedic debate, by *Pravaahana* (*kshatriya* king), the son of sage *Jeevalan*. He goes to his father and conveys his grief to him. Accompanied by his father, *Gautama*, he goes to the king again with the request to educate them with the higher knowledge he possessed. 'It is *kshatriya*'s right to impart this knowledge as he pleases', so saying, the king is found to have taught them both.

The king but advised him that since the knowledge of *Brahman* is so secretive and confidential in nature, one should have gone through long penances before learning that. He further added: ' Hey, *Gautama*, although you happen to be a great scholar yourself, you came to me like an as-yet-uninitiated man seeking knowledge. But what I did was not exactly right. Because this knowledge has never been passed on to a *Brahmin* any time previously and its secret has remained with the *kshatriya* all these ages. That's the reason why I said that the authority to impart this knowledge had always remained with the *kshatriya*'. So saying he imparted the knowledge to them.

The story of Sri *Shuka* (*Brahmin*) receiving the *Brahmic* knowledge from *Janaka*, the *kshatriya* king of *Mithila*, is well known. *Janaka* is one who knows well the principle of *Brahman*. Sri *Shuka*'s father advises him to go to *Janaka* for further education. *Janaka* makes him wait at his gates while pondering if the new pupil was an eligible candidate for such education. On meeting *Janaka* finally, *Shuka* asks: How did this relentless flow of *Samsara* (Universe in its myriad ways) start in the first place? How is it going to end? Advise me on the reality of this spectacle. Your explanation should calm my mind and set all my doubts at rest'.

Janaka replies: 'The moment you are able to believe with firm conviction that this universe is nothing but a grand illusion and dispel all thoughts about it from your mind, know yourself that you have reached the state of Absolute Enlightenment. In that state, you have achieved whatever is there to be achieved. Henceforth, do not ever doubt if you have attained Liberation. Because, you already have'.

Listening to these words, Sri *Shuka* got freed from all cares, bonds and doubts and attained absolute peace in his much-sought-after merger with the Ultimate Truth.(*Mahopanishad*-chap2)

In an earlier era, there used to be a particularly noxious practice of casting the ones who lost in a one-on-one contest on Vedic theory into the sea to die. In one such episode, sage *Ashtaavakra*'s father , *Kahola*, too suffered the same fate along with a few other sages at the hands of *Vaaruni*. In revenge, *Ashtaavakra* defeated *Vaaruni* in a similar contest and was about to cast him into the waters when he saved himself by bringing back to life all those who were similarly sent to their deaths by him in the past. At this success of his , *Ashtaavakra* grew too haughty and in order to tame him there appeared a heavenly Yogini (a lady *yogi* or Sidha) who not only defeated *Ashtaavakra* but on being requested to teach asked him to get his clarifications from *Janaka*, the *kshatriya* king. Thereupon, he proceeds to meet *Janaka* and gets the required advice from him. This story is narrated in the work, *Tripura rahasya, Jnana kanda.*

In the light of the above examples, the view that *kshatriya* can not don the robe of a vedic teacher has to be held as wrong.

In *Chandogya*, 4th chapter, there is this well known story of *Jaanashruti* which goes to prove that even *sudras* used to receive Vedic education from reputed masters. The story goes like this.

One day *Jaanashruti* was relaxing at his mansion when three heavenly swans flew down and started to converse among themselves. One was heard telling: ' *Jaanashruti* is indeed great'. To this, the other replies: 'How is it that one who lacks *Brahmic* knowledge could be great. There is this *Raikva* who alone is really great'. Hearing this, *Jaanashruti* resolves to make good his deficiency by receiving the required knowledge from *Raikva* himself and approaches him with a huge gift made up of six hundred cows, gold jewellery and a chariot and makes the request. But *Raikva* refuses to teach him and snubs him with the words 'Hey, *sudra*, have your gifts to yourself'. A crest fallen *Jaanashruti* goes back to *Raikva* a second time with a much greater package of gifts which included one thousand cows, gold ornaments, a chariot and most importantly his own daughter and an entire village. The gift of the girl meant to serve as *Raikva*'s spouse did turn the tables on *Raikva* who receives all the gifts and teaches *Jaanashruti* the Knowledge , seated as he was at the foremost among holy places, namely, '*Raikva* parna country' gifted to him by *Jaanashruti*.

The attempt made subsequently through five sutras of Brahmasutra and its commentaries to present *Jaanashruti* who was a born-*sudra* as a kshtriya is baseless for the following reason.

The very first time *Jaanashruti* meets him, *Raikva* addresses him as *sudra*, while refusing to be his teacher. Remember that those were days *sudras* were barred from getting Vedic initiation. Had he been really not a *sudra*, *Jaanashruti* would have immediately protested and enlightened *Raikva* about his real caste. But he did not do that. It only goes to prove that *Jaanashruti* was indeed a born-*sudra* and the *sudra* word did not possess any other meaning as claimed by the commentators.

Even a plain reading of the story would tell that *sudra*-word carried the meaning of *sudra*-caste only. Even the commentators knew that people would understand that word only that way. That is why they chose to go through complicated contortions themselves to give the word a different meaning that is deduced and indirect. This in itself would prove that *Jaanashruti* had indeed understood the *sudra*-word as 'born-*sudra*'.

If he went away taking the indirect/deduced meaning (that he was a sorrowful person) of the word, it is quite improbable, because a person who felt hurt at the words of the swan and decided to make good his defect by getting new knowledge, would not have had the required literal knowledge and shrewdness to arrive at the indirect meaning of the *sudra*-word. This also proves *Jaanashruti* was a born-*sudra* and the indirect meaning assigned was something uncalled for.

Again, if indeed he was not a *sudra* but only a *Kshatriya* as argued by the commentators, then he would have straightaway become eligible for receiving lessons. In that case what was the need for him to be turned away by *Raikva*? None, certainly. If there is some rule that excludes the sorrowful from receiving lessons, it would be most unfair. The man with the sorrow which would not go away unless taught and which constitutes the cause of the first rejection is getting imparted with the very knowledge on his second visit. There is also a principle that an aspirant sorrowful about his ignorance is the fittest one to be taught.

If it was to further check his suitability, then there was no need for that for a man like *Raikva* who was in possession of divining powers. If such a testing was indeed unavoidable, it would only mean that *Raikva* did not have such powers and *sudra* word was not used in its '*Yogam*'(deduced) meaning viz. the 'the one who is sorrowful'.

If it was meant to improve upon the aspirant's learning skills, it should have been done by letting him live there for quite some time followed by careful observations. It was also not done. Was it then done with the aim of extracting a higher *dakshina*(gifts) from the aspirant?

He did not even have the power of forethought to guess that, even if refused first , he would have to accede to his request next. It could only mean *Raikva* did not foresee anything with his inner eye, but only saw things with his mortal eyes. He had taught him when he returned with a much larger offer of gifts. He had no qualms about it. It only means that he was greedy after wealth and he was not a man of his word and was not honorable enough to want to keep the sanctity of his own word. All this points to the one and only fact that the *sudra*-word he used meant only born-*sudra* and it did not carry any derived meaning as assigned by later-day commentators.

(*What follows is the relevant portions of Sri Sankara's commentary that appear word-for-word in both the works 'Ancient Malayalam' and this book. The explanation for the terms carrying suffixes need to be looked up in 'Ancient Malayalam', which finds a place in this collection itself)*

"Sutra[34] 34 :

Just because man is entitled to knowledge, there is a view that *sudra* is also entitled to knowledge in the same way as the gods are entitled to it. This is just to dispel this notion.

Sudra has the right to knowledge. There appears to be no denial of access to knowledge to a *sudra* in the same way he is denied sacrificial rights. It is true that he lacks '*Agnituam*[35]'. It only bars him from performing sacrifices. But it does not deny him access to the knowledge of it. Nor does it imply that he is incapable of learning such stuff. When *Jaanashruti* approaches *Raikva* for knowledge, the *Sudra*-word he utters while insulting him by saying, 'Hey *Sudra*, keep your cows to yourself' becomes a subject of much debate. Though *Vidura* etc were born *sudras* they were considered eligible for knowledge acquisition. On the basis of the above-stated reasons, if *sudra* becomes eligible for knowledge, then I have to say this. Just because *Sudras* have no right whatsoever over Vedas, they can not seek to acquire knowledge of it. Those who studied Vedas alone can have the right to interpreting its meanings. *Sudra* can not learn Vedas because they do not go through the rites of passage like *Upa*n*ayana*[36], which is only the prerogative of *Brahmins, kshatriyas* and *vaishyas*. When he lacks eligibility, the craving for knowledge alone can not constitute the basis of his right to knowledge. Since he is denied knowledge, he stands denied of the eligibility for it too. By whichever rule he becomes ineligible for sacrifice, by the same rule he stands ineligible for knowledge.

Just because *sudra*-word occurs in the story, one can not think *sudra* is entitled to knowledge. Not only that, it relates only to the *sudra* who appears in the narrative. Because the words of the swan (quoted above) makes him sorrowful. Here when he is addressed as *sudra* by *Raikva, Raikva* only means the knowledge-seeker was sorrowful.(because the *sudra*-word has the meaning, 'one who is sorrowful' also). And he did not use it as meaning '*sudra*-by-birth'.

Sutra 35:

According to this sutra too, *Jaanashruti* is not a born-*sudra*. Because towards the second part of the *Jaanashruti* story, due to the association with the name of *Chaitraratha*, the *kshatriya*, *Jaanashruti* too looks like belonging to the *kshatriya* race for different reasons. Because of this reason too, the born-*sudra* does not become eligible for knowledge.

Sutra 36.

According to this rule too, *Jaanashruti* is not entitled to knowledge. It is established that for initiation into knowledge, the aspirant should have gone through *upanayana* etc. It is evident from the following example. *Bharadwajis,* in search of the knowledge of *Brahman,* approached '*Pipalaadan*' who is like god himself. At that time these words were heard: 'Do not give them *upanayana*'. It only shows *upanayana* is a prime requirement before imparting knowledge. Based on this saying that '*Sudra* is the fourth *varna* and a single caste', and also because he is not required to go through *upanayana* etc on account of his being without sin, it is established that he need not go through the rites of passage like *upanayana.*

Sutra 37:

This also tells that *sudra* has no right to knowledge. *Jaabala* was given *upanayana* and imparted knowledge by sage *Gautama*n only after getting him to swear on oath that he was not a *sudra.* But the fact of the matter is that none other than a *Brahmin* could make such a statement of discrimination.

Sutra 38:

This sutra too bars *Sudra* from knowledge. According to *Smritis, sudra* can neither listen to nor acquire knowledge of the Vedas. This should naturally include a bar on interpreting and practicing the Vedas. There is a rule which says: ' As he had listened to the Vedas, let his ears be plugged by pouring molten lead and wax'. Not only that, there is another rule which says that if a *sudra* utters veda, his tongue should be chopped off and if he carries the veda in his person, his body should be cut open. Also the veda clearly prohibits imparting of knowledge to the *sudra* and asserts that teaching, sacrifice and gifts by way of charity are meant for *Brahmins* only. And therefore it has to be concluded that *sudra* can not claim vedic knowledge as a matter of right."

(The extract from' *Ancient Malayalam*' ends)

The story of *Jaabala* is one chosen as an example in the above commentaries and which is considered as strong an evidence as *Jaanashruti*'s. We will discuss it briefly here.

Jaabala goes to sage *Gautama* for receiving *Brahmic* knowledge. But *Gautama* harbours doubts about the person's caste. But he proceeds to impart the knowledge after making *Jaabala* swear on oath that he was not a *sudra*.

That *sudra* can not be taught Vedas is an accepted fact. *Jaabala* approaches the master just for acquiring that knowledge. From the fact that he gets him to swear that he was not a *sudra*, it is clear that *Gautama* had doubts about his caste. Besides, *sudras* are considered untruthful in behavior. But *Gautama* just takes his word as truth. When *Gautama* could have made further enquiries and confirmed *Jaabala*'s caste, he chooses not to do so and readily agrees to teach him the ultimate knowledge sought, on the strength of a mere oath that could have been very well false. This also goes to prove the following things. That *Gautama* was not particularly strict about not teaching him. That he did not believe that either he or *Jaabala* comes to harm on account of it. That he did not believe that *sudras* were strictly forbidden to receive vedic education.

Explanation: But the question remains as to why he got *Jaabala* to swear.

Rebuttal : It must have been done just as an excuse to be presented before his peers of the day who were very particular about adhering to their self-made rules like '*sudras* can not learn and *sudras* should not be taught' as if those rules were so sacred that they can not be flouted.

In case *Gautama* was taken to task and questioned on this score, he could always explain that he taught *Jaabala* only after ascertaining his caste by getting him to swear about it.

Sri *Sankara Bhagavadpadar* himself, in his commentary on the very first of the sutras of Brahmasutra, says: ' Going through *Upanayana* and possessing hands-on knowledge of sacrificial rites are not pre-conditions for following the path of Liberation/Self Realization. The only requirement is that the person must possess a certain 'quartet of instruments or means' called '*Saadhana chatushtayam*[6]', irrespective of the order in which one follows the other.

But it is baffling that contrary to his own expressed view, given above, the *Bhagavadpadar*himself had stipulated the order in which the above things should happen, in his aforementioned commentaries on sutras 34 to 38.

He starts off on the sutra 1 with a discussion on the word '*Adha*[7]' occurring in it. This word has four different meanings, among which 'afterwards' is one. While declaring all the other three meanings as irrelevant to the context and reiterating the dispensability of prior formal vedic learning for self realisation, he sets about answering a hypothetical question as to what exactly is the requirement to be had before one sets himself forth on the path of self realisation. The requirement is the attainment of a 'quartet of instruments or means' by the aspirant.

They are: 1)The capacity to discriminate between the real and the unreal 2) Total disregard for the pleasures of this world and the after-worlds , 3) A set of six qualities consisting of independence from the five sensory organs and the five executive organs, non-attachment, endurance, faith, and concentration, and finally 4) yearning for Enlightenment.

The work '*Aitareya Brahmanam*' mentions about one forest-dweller cum game-hunter called '*Kavasha*', who happened to possess a deep knowledge of the Veda and was a regular participant in *Yajnas* alongside sages.

On the banks of the river '*Saraswati*', preparations were on for the conduct of a *Yajna* (sacrificial fire). *Kavasha*, the tribal hunter born of a low-caste mother, appeared there suddenly raising the hackles of those assembled who not only drove him out , but put him in a desert to ensure that he did not even get water to drink. Thus deprived of food and water, he sat and composed fifteen hymns in praise of God, which brought him divine blessings and the river "*Saraswati*' changed course and veered around to flow by him in close proximity. Learning about the surprising developments, the sages came over to the place, took him back to the sacrificial grounds and conducted the *yajna* called '*Aponaptriya*'. The hymns he composed were called '*Aponaptriya* hymns' and they found a place in the Veda.

When the hymn composed by a hunter could find a place in the Veda, who, one would ask, is not eligible to study the Veda?

This story finds mention in the '*Kaushitaki Brahmanam*' too. It goes like this.

The sages *Gritsamada, Visvamitra, Vaamadeva, Athri, Bharadwaja, and Vasishta* were preparing to begin a sacrifice (*Yajna*) on *Saraswati*'s banks. *Kavasha* arrived there and seated himself among the sages. They insulted him by calling him 'the son of a housemaid' and refused to even eat with him. *Kavasha*n got furious. He approached *Saraswati*'s banks, composed the above hymns and received divine grace. Goddess *Saraswati* accompanied him. At this point, the sages reached the conclusion that *Kavasha*n was devoid of sin and impurity. They asked of him for forgiveness: 'O great sage, salutations to thee. You are the most respected amongst us for the reason that the Goddess Herself had accompanied you. Kindly do not ever cause any worry to us'. Then they made him a main priest of the sacrifice and pacified him. That is *Kavasha*'s greatness. He became known in the name of his hymn.

Again, in the Veda itself there is the story of '*Kakshivaan*', a *sudra* by birth. There is a prayer wherein *Kakshivan* finds mention in glowing terms.

'Oh, *Brahmanaspati*, kindly make me, a drinker of the *Soma* spirit, too as resplendent a man as *Kakshivaan*, the son of a woman called '*Ushik*'.

All in all, it remains without doubt that people born as *sudras* are as much entitled to the Vedas as anybody else, both in learning and practicing it.

Naturally, the Veda can not be expected to contain principles contrary in content to the core message of the above stories. *Jaiminiya* sutra has this to say. That practices/ideas that are running counter to the contents of *Srutis* will not get any support from the *Srutis* is all too obvious. *Meemamsa*[8] says that such practices running afoul of the message of the *Srutis* should be considered as unwarranted, baseless and deserving of no respect. If there are lines in the Veda in the nature of holding an opposite view, *Manusmriti*provides a solution . It says that when there are two mutually contradictory views/methods found mentioned in the Veda itself, both should be accorded the same importance. Therefore, even if the Veda declares in one place that *Kshatriya* is ineligible for teaching while the *sudra* is for learning, one can categorically believe that *Kshatriya* can teach and *sudra* can take lessons, on the strength of such precedents as mentioned above that are accepted by all.

-4-

Instances of flouting/tweaking of tenets

(Pramanantara vicharam)

To quote from *Manu*:

'Let all the three castes (*Brahmin, kshatriya, vaishya*)with their designated duties learn. What is to be ensured is that the teacher should not be a non-*brahmin*. Let the *Brahmin* decide the means of livelihood of all. Even as he does so, let him perform his duties too.'

This is all it says. But nowhere is it specifically or explicitly mentioned that *sudra* should not learn the Veda. To explain it further, since man can not be expected to do everything that he needs to, all by himself, there came about the allocation of duties, from the earliest beginnings . Like what existed as kings, priests, *'petricher'(patricians or nobles),' plevier'* (*plebeians*) in Rome and as kings, priests, lords, and commons in England; here too, much before all that, the four caste system came into being with their respective allocation of duties. Imparting vedic knowledge is *brahmin*'s duty; protecting the land from enemies, the *kshatriya*'s; doing commerce in the necessaries of life, the *vaishya*'s; and serving all the three castes in a master-servant relationship, that of the *sudra*'s. *Manu* does not detect any flaw on the part of someone pursuing the path of Liberation away from worldly affairs, even as he performs his entrusted duties. *Smritis*too do not seem to object to it. On the off chance they do, they are subject to the *Sruti* principles.

Whatever info is not found in the Veda can be had from the Smriti. Those that are not found in both can be learnt from *Puranas*. When the three are contradicting one another, *Smriti*s are more trustworthy than *Puranas* and the

Veda more trustworthy than the Smriti.

When the Veda and *Smriti*are in conflict with each other, one has to go by the Veda. When they do not contradict, both are equally acceptable.

Any view *Smritis*and *Puranas* take contrary to the Veda should be rejected. *Puranas* remain handy to explain/ justify anything and everything. But anything in it which disagrees with what the Veda says should be rejected straightaway. There is no use, debating the right or wrong of it.

It is now time to think of an aphorism that is often cited by those who maintain that *sudra* can not learn the Veda.

'*Na stree Sudrow Vedam Adheeyataam*'.

This is neither Veda nor *Smriti*. It is just a sutra. It does not come under *Puranas*, epics or even tradition. So, there is no need to accept it . Nor it deserves to be condemned. The meaning of those words is this. '*Sudra*s and women do not need to study'. It does not mean : '*sudra*s and women should not study'.

If in course of time, if someone chose to emphasise the second of the two meanings as its real meaning, he can not be blamed. Because, down the ages, it was the practice of those that interpreted ancient texts to give it a spin to suit the demands of the times. That is, they were forced to read unintended meanings in straightforward phrases.

To cite a couple of instances of such aberrations:

This is from the work '*Paraashara smriti*'. It says in one place:

'Nashte mrute pravrajite
Kleebe cha pathithe pathow
Pancha swaapalsu naareenaam
Pathiranyo vidheeyate'.

‘ Women are free to marry again when the husband is permanently far and away, or dead, or has taken to *sanyas* (renouncement), or is eunich-like, or is of degraded character’. But *Sri Madhava Acharya* who interpreted the work side-steps this stanza by claiming that it is ‘*yugaandara vishayam*’(pertaining to some other *yuga*).

In *Yajnavalkya* smriti, it is said in one stanza: ‘ A married woman can marry another person, if she finds that person to be better than her husband’. It again says in another stanza: ‘Such a woman will be called a *Punarbhoo*, irrespective of whether she had reached puberty or not’. *Vignanesvara* who interpreted the work later, while ignoring the second of the stanzas, interprets the first as meaning something different.

*Manusmriti*declares the age of twelve as the most ideal age for a girl’s marriage, while eight as much less so (*gaunapaksham*). Its interpreter *Kalluka bhata* totally omits this portion and misinterprets that the stanza deals with the age of man only. Commentaries/interpretations are meant to make difficult subjects easy, not to distort even clear ones with a mischievous intent.

Let us again take the line, ‘*na stree sudrow vedam adheeyate*’. The last word in it ,*adheeyatam*, has different meanings. But we are now concerned with whether to take it as meaning ‘ should not’ or as ‘need not’. In such questions, the rule of thumb is that the meaning that does not run counter to ‘*gurutharapramanangal*’(established tenets) should be taken as correct. For that, let us consider the story of a woman named ‘*Gargi*’ from *Brihadaranyaka Upanishad*. She was learned enough to debate Vedic questions with great sage-scholars like *Yajnavalkya*.

Gargi, the daughter of *Vachaknava*, who had stayed away after the debate in the sixth' *Brahmanam*[9] spoke thus: 'O most honourable sages, Just listen to me. If you permit me, I will ask two questions to this *Yajnavalkya*. If he is able to answer them correctly, none of you will win a contest with him'.

They gave her the permission to ask. She then addressed *Yajnavalkya*, thus: 'Like a courageous king getting ready with his arrows on his bow to fight, I will shoot two questions to you. You should answer them'. *Yajnavalkya* said: 'Ask away'.

Gargi asks: 'What is on the upper and lower sides of the hemisphere of subtle-ethereal higher worlds? What is it that separates this earth from these worlds? On what is this duality, ever-present in the past, the present, and the future, supporting itself'?

If the story of this woman engaging, in a debate, the great *Yajnavalkya* , unbeatable even by the likes of *Aasvalan, Aartabhagan, Bhyujyu, Ushastan, Kaholan* etc, could form the subject matter of an *Upanishad*, then do we require any further evidence to conclude that women too have right to the Vedas?

Again, in the very same *Brihadaranyaka Upanishad*, 4th chapter, 5th*Brahmanam*, there is this story of *Maitreyi*, one of the two wives of *Yajnavalkya*. Of the two, *Maitreyi* was of a spiritual bent of mind and so a seeker after the Ultimate Truth and had indeed attained the state of Bliss. *Yajnavalkya*, suddenly, decides to take to a life of total renunciation and hence plans to partition his properties equally between his two wives. Mitreyi asks if she would get liberation from mortal existence even if she gets the entire earth as her share. *Yajnavalkya* answers with an emphatic NO. ' In that case, give me knowledge of the *brahman*', she pleads. *Yajnavalkya* accedes to her request and imparts to her the asked-for secret knowledge.

Stories of both women who excelled in Vedic knowledge find place in the very Veda itself. It is, therefore, but natural to conclude that the Veda was not at all a taboo to womenfolk.

Under the circumstances, there appears to be no need to cite instances of women reciting Vedic mantras meant for them during the conduct of *Yajnas*.

'*ShatapataBrahmanam*, in its description of the '*Dashapurnamasa* sacrifice' prescribes a specific *mantra* (incantation) for *sudras*, at the time ghee is poured into the fire, alongside the *mantra* for *Brahmins* and *kshatriyas*, for recital. It also prescribes other incantations for *sudras* during the performance of the same sacrifice.

In *Sukla Yajur* veda's 28th chapter, there is an invocation wishing for someone who would teach the Veda to others with the specific aim of benefiting all, namely the *Brahmins*, *kshatriyas*, *vaishyas*, *sudras*, friends and even foes alike.

'*Apastambam smriti*' declares that only those practices which are sanctioned by and in accordance with the Veda can be called the right practices. All this proves that Veda used to be learnt by whoever fancied learning it.

To go back to the aphorism and its interpretations mentioned in the beginning, in the light of the above observations, it goes without saying that the meaning which should be considered as correct is the one which says 'women and *sudras* do not need to study', which do not at all impose a blanket ban on them studying the veda, unlike the other interpreted meaning, and which in effect amounts to repudiating the Veda itself.

We have so far examined only the scriptural anecdotes and connected evidence, both in favour and against. Now, we will ponder rational questions.

-5-

Reasoning it out

Does it at least stand to reason to say that 'the *sudra* should not learn the Veda'. Any religious text of importance is likely to assert that the two fundamental requirements for attaining Enlightenment are a righteous life and an awareness about one's own self and the Cosmic self.

Bhagavad Gita says:

'After going through countless births, the one who had come to possess the Truest Knowledge reaches me'.

The *Upanishads* say:

'The one who has acquired such Knowledge overcomes Death'.

'The one who identifies himself with his soul alone will live in everlasting happiness', so proclaims the Veda.

To say that *sudra* should not acquire the knowledge related to Enlightenment could only mean that *sudra* should never attain the enlightened state. If only this rule had been strictly adhered to in the past, does it not mean that no *sudra* would have ever attained Enlightenment. Will any one agree with that? However, is it also not a fact that even the learned *Vaishnavaites* among the *Brahmins*, who pride themselves on their divine powers and their ability to move even the heavens with their little fingers, accept that *sudras* such as '*Thirukachinambi*' and '*Thirupaanazhuvar*' have attained *Mukti* (Enlightenment). When asked as to how this had come to pass, they, unable to dispute the Veda on the one hand and refute the fact of their attaining *Mukti* on the other, start mumbling that *sudras* were only barred from learning the Veda and certainly not from internalizing the sense of its messages. Let them ponder on the correctness of their explanation. This could only mean that Vedic recitation or more correctly the sound of its articulation is more important than its underlying meanings. How could one accept that a box is more valuable than the precious stones it contains. Are not sounds related to their meanings the way the box is to its contents. Offered with the option of choosing either the stones or its container, if some one prefers the container to the gems, will he not be considered as beyond insane? Let us proceed to see what the Veda itself has to say on the correspondence between its word and its sound.

According to *Rigveda* itself, one who recites the Veda without understanding its meaning is equivalent to a pillar supporting the rafters. This statement alone is enough to infer the quality of those who learn the Veda without grasping its meaning. There is no need for quoting more such observations. Even if we agree that the chaff that covers the grain is more important than the grain itself, we have to examine if this practice was existing from the beginning. It is believed that even the *Brahmin* who denies the Veda to the *sudra* will not deny him the study of the epics and *Puranas*. But, alas, *Puranas* often carry lines from the Veda itself. We would only mention two such instances.

The first one is from The *Mahabharat, Adi parva,* 3rd chapter.

'*Devavaswinou vagfi rigfi:*'

The second one is from '*Sakunthalopakhyanam*", 74th chapter'.

One wonders how *sudra* could study vedic lines that *Puranas* carry while he can't read them in their original. Or is it that the *sudra* should not read the *purana* too. But the fact remains that many of the authors of *Puranas* were *sudras*. For instance, the author of '*Soota samhita*' was a *sudra*. Does the importance of the work suffer any diminution on account of this fact? Not at all. When asked why, the routine reply is that such authors were great personalities and so there was no kind of ban, whatsoever, on them. But is it not their erudition that fetched them greatness? Learning is certainly not taxed by the government. The path of learning is the same for all. Is it not by following that path the '*Alwars*' and '*Naayanmars*'[10] attained greatness. So, even today, is there any doubt that most of the *sudras* would shine with such greatness if only they follow the same path?

Sage *Paraashara*, the son of a boat- woman, and sage *Vyasa*, the son of a fisherwoman have authored the Vedas. But they were considered *Brahmins*. The answer, when questioned, is that one should not seek after the origin of sages and rivers. People are apt to take refuge under such adages when they run out of explanations. The fact of the matter is that both of them were born of lowly wombs. They became *Brahmins* because their fathers were *Brahmins*. Let us see if at least this principle holds. If it holds, *Pandu* , *Dhritarashtra* and *Vidura* , the sons of *Vyasa*, the *Brahmin*, should have been *Brahmins*. But on the basis of their mothers' caste, if *Pandu* and *Dhritarashtra* became *Kshatriyas* how is it that *Vidura* became a *sudra*. If such questions are decided on the basis of one's mother's caste, then *Vyasa* and *Paraashara* should have been considered as non-*brahmins*. If you differentiate between *Vyasa* and *Paraashara* , both born of proper matrimony, on the one hand and *Pandu*, *Dhritarashtra* and *Vidura* born of their mother's deviant sexuality on the other, how is it that those who lost *brahmin*hood did not lose the right to Vedic education ? Because it is clearly said that they got Vedic education. Or if sperm (father) is the deciding factor, then all those born of low caste mothers to *Brahmin* fathers should be entitled to vedic education in their capacity of being *Brahmins*. That in other words should mean that those that are born of proper wedlock can not learn the Veda while those that are born out of adulterous unions can.

Let us leave it aside and examine if the '*brahmin*hood', that invests one with the right to learn and teach the Veda , is acquired through birth alone, *Jnana*(knowledge) alone, *karma*(action) alone, and *Brahmic* knowledge alone or a combination of all that. In case it is birth that decides, is it enough to have just a *Brahmin* father, whoever may be the mother? Or just a *Brahmin* mother , whatever be the father's caste? Or is it that both should be *Brahmins*? In the first case, you can not critique it if the children of a *Brahmin* father born to his low-caste paramour go thru the rites of passage meant for *Brahmins*. It will be equally applicable to children born of *Nair* mothers to *Brahmin* fathers. In the second case, it would be certainly wrong to denounce at least some of them out there as courtesan's progeny. The third case should render even *Vyasa* and *Paraashara* as non-*brahmins*. As it is established practice that someone born of *Brahmin* parents continue to remain a *Brahmin* even after he gets excommunicated for some reason, so it follows that even those *Brahmins* who convert to other faiths, eat meat, cohabit with lowly women and generally live in contravention of all tenets of *brahmin*hood should also be accepted as *Brahmins*. But if the atrophy in conduct should divest one of *brahmin*hood, then we have to accept that it is not birth but his innate nature and action/conduct that decides his caste.

That is why *Vajrasoochika Upanishad* says:

Janmanaa jaayate *sudra*:

Karmanaa jaayate dwija:

(By birth, everyone is a *sudra*. Thereafter depending upon the activity he chooses, one becomes *Brahmin* or *kshatriya* or *Vaishya*.)

While on this subject, the attributes that earn one *brahmin*hood have to be examined carefully. It is to be seen whether they consist of mere formalities like his going through the rites of passage or of his deeds/action both good and foul. If it is the former, even *sudras* who choose to go through such formalities should become *Brahmins*. If it is the latter, all *Brahmins* who do not follow their *Dharma* will have to be considered as non-*brahmins* and all those who are *sudras* by appearance but are practitioners of *brahmini*cal virtues will become *Brahmins*. In the matter of propensities displayed towards eschewing evils such as falsehood, homicide, jealousy etc and adopting such virtues as truthfulness, compassion, righteousness etc, we do not find any perceptible differences between *Brahmins* and *sudras*. Accordingly, *Brahmins* do not possess any additional advantage over others, nor the *sudras* any deficiency. Some may tend to opine that inborn nature cum action is just not sufficient unless it goes with birth. But, sage *Viswamitra*, a confirmed *kshatriya* by birth, became a *Brahmin* purely on account of his inborn nature and action. Similarly, '*Kavasha*' who was *sudra* by birth became not only a *Brahmin* but rose to be a *rishi* (sage) of repute, for the same reason.

Not only that, *Aitareya Brahmanam* says that a *Kshatriya* failing to abide by his designated protocol and taking to that of a *Brahmin* will actually be a *Brahmin* and further proceeds to inform that such a thing had actually happened. It further says: ' Even a *kshatriya* arriving at a sacrificial ground as a *brahmin* donning the attire of a *Brahmin* and carrying the necessary implements in readiness to perform the *Yajna* is eligible to participate in the *Yajna*'.

Again, to quote from the same work: 'Wearing the skin of a deer, adherence to the rules of renouncement, service by the *Brahmins* themselves etc will make a *Brahmin* out of a *kshatriya* who had taken a vow of *brahmin*hood'

Naturally, a *sudra* who takes to the daily routines and practices of a *brahmin* should also become a *brahmin*. If that does not happen, it would mean that *brahmin*hood is got neither through birth nor rites of passage. If it is got on the basis of attainment of knowledge of *Brahman*, nobody is going to fault it. Even then, having the Knowledge but not the connected activities is going to be of no avail.

A line from *Uttara gita* of *Mahabharata* is worth quoting here.

'A *Brahmin*, well-versed in the Veda but not practising his *dharma* is a *Brahmin*-donkey'.

Since *Brahmic* knowledge and its practice have nothing much to do with birth, they are attainable goals for all. May be obtaining absolute perfection in that enterprise is not possible. But, without doubt, achieving as much perfection as a *Brahmin* by birth possibly can is within the realm of possibility of *sudras*. Is it not, therefore, possible for *sudras* too to learn the Veda like the *Brahmins*? If birth along with Vedic knowledge and its practice has got to be a necessary condition for *brahmin*hood, the revered *Alwars* who suffer from the taint of lowly births could have never become *Brahmins*. Likewise, those who totally gave up all the traditions/practices like the '*smarta madhva* seers' and those who partially gave up the same like the

Vaishnavasi will not be *Brahmins*. And also those who don *brahmins*' robes without possessing the *Brahmic* knowledge will also lose *Brahminhood.* This discourse leads us to the inescapable conclusion that nobody out there in the world could consider himself as eligible to learn the Veda. But from among this ineligible lot, if a few manage to learn the Veda by falsely pretending that they are eligible, what exactly is the harm in letting others who are genuinely interested also to learn it. And, therefore, it is our contention that either all should be eligible or all should be ineligible. There just can't be a some-can-and-some-can't stipulation.

Suppose, owing to scrupulous observance of traditions/ practices, some are empowered to learn, let us examine it a little.

According to *Jamadagni Samhita,* there were four castes in *Treta yuga*; but in *Kali yuga*, *Kshatriya* and *Vaishya* went off the list. This principle was established by *Brahmins* themselves. *Kerala Avakashakramam*itself leaves out *Kshatriyas* and *vaishyas* while listing out the sixty four castes. Accordingly, we need to take into account only *Brahmins* and *sudras* while deliberating on this.

Consider the *brahmins*-by-birth category. One can be absolutely sure that, among them, there would be none who practises all the routines and duties and observes all the traditions etc as prescribed by masters like *Manu* in their entirety. Even if there is some exception to this observation somewhere, the majority of them are like that. Naturally they should all, undoubtedly, lose their *brahmin*-status. It makes no difference at all whether the loss of *brahminhood* had happened due to breach of rules or basic ineligibility. That would lead to a condition where there are no Brahmins left in the society. Even if it is so, it will not be entirely pointless to have a caste there, whatever be the name by which it is known. In that case, as told before, it leads to a state where either all become eligible or no one is eligible for learning the Veda. If learning by certain ineligible people can be approved of, how is it possible to fault the others who too do just that? To those who are devoid of all vanity and engaged in serious study of the Veda, this will appear ridiculous.

Lastly, supposing there is a rule prohibiting all *sudra*s from eating all kinds of food, will it be practically enforceable or acceptable to them. Like food is a basic requirement of this life, *Jnana* (Knowledge) is , not only to life in this world, but also to the other worlds. How is it that such a basic need could be denied to *sudra*s. Such denial could have only two possible reasons. One is that the upper class is afraid that it would lose their pre-eminent position in society. The second could be their obstinacy about *sudra*s submitting themselves unquestioningly to all their unfair diktats. Naturally such a rule can not be held as fair or valid. Even Christians and Muslims let all study their scriptures. So, why should anyone assume that the Veda is going to get polluted or something, if *sudra*s touch it. The fact about the Veda is that it is meant to uplift whoever gets to learn it. How is it possible, in that case, for such a powerful document as the Veda to suffer any degradation if *sudra* learns it. Of course, *Sudra*'s position in society today is lowly and degraded. But that does not mean , some day in future, they are not going to occupy positions of stature and power. And, therefore, it should be accepted that all that is required for Vedic learning is only right desire and conduct on the part of the aspirant. If one who refuses food to the starving can be called inhuman, what would you call one who refuses the Veda to the deserving. Even extreme cruelty when practiced on a regular and daily basis will begin to appear like harmless routine, like it is in the case of a butcher. Imparting Vedic knowledge to all without any obstinacy or rigidity about it should be regarded as a just and right practice and an act of extreme compassion and it should accordingly be practiced as such.

(ends)

CHAPTER TWO

The Place of Woman and Man in the World

(Prapanchatil Stree purushanmaarude Staanam)

Primal Nature (*Moola prakruti*) and the Supreme Cosmic Consciousness (*Brahma chaitanya*) are beleved to be the mother and father of all life in this universe, whether mobile or immobile. In the presence of *Brahma Chaitanya, Moola Prakruti* acts to engender union/ separation between atoms to bring about the states of Beginning, Middle and the End of all things. That it is this union that had created the universe is evident from an analysis of the syllable or sound represented by the letter 'A' (pronounced as in China). This sound is supposed to be the result of the above union. This sound or syllable is fundamental to the entire world of sounds, letters and words that follow. In most languages the written form of this sound is supposed to reflect this union. It will have two parts, the upper part representing the male Cosmic Consciousness and the lower part representing the female Primal Nature. Separated from each other, each loses its gender and ability to create . When they unite, as in sound 'A', a whole world of sounds/ words gets created. In course of time, this fact got concealed from public knowledge. Because, upon development of languages, this fact had to be either concealed or there was no incentive for remembering it.

Like the upper and lower parts of this sound in the world of all letters are male and female in gender representing the divine *Shiva* and *Shakti* aspects (Cosmic consciousness and Primal nature), each living being is born of the union of a father and a mother who are responsible for its creation, sustenance and dissolution.. In the continued engagement of the two, what is born survives and birth multiplies. And in their disengagement, creation stops and when the two work at cross purposes and are in conflict with each other, what is created disintegrates. Since, except in association with the Cosmic consciousness, the Primal nature does not possess the power to perform, the former is generally considered to be the more important of the two. But it can not be so, for the following reason. Since, it is the Primal nature that provides the initial space for the Supreme consciousness to turn on the trigger and the consequent acts of creation, sustenance and dissolution that follow are also entirely the work of Primal nature, it stands to reason to conclude that Primal nature should be considered the more important of the two. It was told that it is the *Brahman*(cosmic consciousness) that impels primal nature towards creating the universe. But , alas, what is created does not entitle *Brahman* to the enjoyment of it or bestows on Him the right over it. Nor is *Brahman* having any interest or pride in the creation. All belongs to Primal nature and her progeny. Though the relation between the female and the male is symbiotic in nature, the role of the male is really one of a passive partner. Like the *Brahman,* through his presence, enabling *Shakti* to create the universe, man in union with the female creates each of the little body-universes and keeps the wheel of life moving. He does not have to go through the travails of pregnancy and running of the household. Nor is the build of his body suited for those purposes. In the practical world, pain, hardships and responsibilities are more for the woman. Social progress or decline also has a bearing on woman's managerial skills. Therefore, in the above two aspects of life, woman happens to be the more important. Man is created to protect his kin and provide for them as part of his responsibility by enduring , if need be, all hardships like roaming about in wildernesses for earning the daily bread.

But, the woman is granted a special power. She, while stationed at home, through her sheer will power and efficiency administers and manages not only the home but through the home the entire world itself justly as if through the exercise of some magical charm. In the helpful presence of man, the woman transcends the whole world as an absolute authority of sorts over the three worlds[1].

Instead of that, if some men are prone to pronounce that '*na stree swatantryam arhati*'(women do not deserve freedom) and practise accordingly by treating her as a caged bird and as an instrument for making babies, keeping her in ignorance, bondage and slavishness, and acting arrogantly as if he alone matters, then it is unfair, unjust and against the order of nature. This does not mean that men who are holding jobs like administering the affairs of the country should quit and take up household duties. Nor does it mean that women who should spread their imperceptible power through the world while being stationed at their homes should chuck it and take up administrative duties or go about addressing gatherings. Her home is a mini-universe in itself and the members of her family are akin to the people who inhabit the earth.

The woman that knows her real role in her setting, and administers it so admirably as to cause all round progress and prosperity there, is in fact the empress of the world. Though she is all-powerful to that extent, providing her with the necessary instruments for discharging her duties is man's responsibility. She need not have to undergo stresses and strains beyond her normal mental and physical capacities.

'More the responsibility, higher the power' is a true dictum. That responsibility is more for woman than for man is undisputed. Even the most hard-hearted man would melt and would prostrate before her if only he ponders for a moment on the sufferings she undergoes in her different roles as wife , mother, sister etc. Also, even the worst misogynist good-for-nothing, endowed with rancor and ingratitude, would agree that woman remains the most sublime example of tireless endurance and meticulous care. Let man with thoughtfulness and thankfulness contemplate hard. Let him take note of her untold hardships and onerous responsibilities. For whom are these honourable beings toiling for? They do not look for even a minor gesture of gratitude from man. How unimportant are all that for them!

She goes through the pregnancy of nearly ten months, suffers labour pains and gives birth to the child. However grotesque and ugly looking the baby may be, she handles its excreta willingly, breastfeeds it and rears it up with care. Even a physically challenged son, who is dependent on his mother for survival but is unkind to her and is in the habit of harassing her constantly in multiple ways , is looked upon by the mother without thoughts of recompense and with feelings of tenderness and prayers for his wellbeing. Where would one find such unqualified greatness except in a mother? There is nothing in this world which is equal to mother's love that is constantly focussed on a son's wellbeing, that too, right from the helpless state of his infancy, during which he had brought in absolutely nothing for his survival and remained so helpless as to do nothing except crying, to possibly the end of his existence. There are some modernists who think that they needed mother's care only until they came of age and it was just the mother's responsibility to give them care and hence they do not owe anything to their moms. To those men without any sense of gratitude, there is only one thing to say: 'Who had in fact called you to this world? If someone did, it was certainly not for as sinister a being as you'. In fact it is the mother who in an inexplicable way is the causative factor for all the good that happens in his life even beyond the stage of infancy. When the son grows up to a stage where the mother can not take care of him anymore, she makes him marry and entrusts the care of her son to that woman. Even then, her thoughts about the son and her anxieties about his welfare do not cease. It is such tender feelings of hers that result in the future well being of the son. Like it is said that it was just God's Will that created everything in the beginning , it is mother's love that enables children to enjoy a life of comforts later on. As a real mother who gave birth at one stage of their lives or in the form of a wife later or the mother who gave birth to her daughter to be his wife and life-partner in later stages, it is the presence of mother's grace that permeates sons' entire lives. Looking at things this way, there can not be two views about the fact that woman's is the more powerful and responsible role than the man's. And, therefore, even when we say that there is no doubt that it is our mother and father who rule over our lives, it is the mother who gets the pride of place. And, it is just as it should be.

The Sanskrit word for husband is '*Bharta*' which means 'one who administers', and that for wife is '*Bhaarya*' which means 'one who is administered'. One can sense a certain impropriety in the description. The reason possibly for man's audacity in calling her so could be the fact that by nature woman is humble and modest and she hence can not be as vociferous as man about her superior power and position.

But it is found that the ancients and other knowledgeable persons have considered woman as the 'number one'. In fact she should have been given the name '*Bharti*' which means 'woman who administers'. The position of the man is like that of *Brahman* who does not play an active part in the matter of creation/sustenance/ destruction. And, hence, according her the name , *Bhaarya*, was stupid to say the least. Because, a woman remains a wife only up to her pregnancy and when she gives birth to a son, it is in a way her man that is born as her son and that is why she is called '*Jaaya*' which means ' the woman in whom one is born'. As the husband himself gets born as her son, the names '*Jaaya*' and 'mother' suits the wife very much. Giving her a name which does little justice to her role is just one example of the misdeeds of men towards women.

Thus, there are two mothers, the biological mother and the mother with conferred motherhood. . Between the two, the superior one is of course the biological mother. Because she had given birth not only to him but to his siblings too. The real mother is unique while the role of invested or assumed motherhood can go to more than one (meaning more than one wife). Assumed-motherhood usually happens but as willed by the real mother only. It is the mother's silent blessings that bring about happiness and wellbeing in children's lives. For the above reasons, mother has to be considered as Mother Goddess or *Shakti* herself (*Moola Prakruti*), and the father who plays a protective and supporting role should get the place of *Brahman*.

What service by way of gratitude could the sons render their mothers who carried them in their wombs, went through labour pains, reared them with love and care, and even bless them silently and diligently every day of their lives. None at all. The utmost one could do is to remember her daily in deep gratitude and pay her silent obeisances. The children who owe their lives to the anxiety, physical stresses, and mental strains of the mothers and the help and presence of the father have their respective duties towards them. But one must remember that his first duty is towards his mother. There is a saying we would do well to remember: '*Janani janmabhumicha swargaadapi gariyasi*'. It means : 'Mother and motherland are nobler than the Heaven'. Even the finest of sons can not hope to do enough justice to his duty to the mother. The children of course have a similar duty towards the father too, but it is only secondary in nature. Third in importance is the home in which one grew up. It must be considered as a real temple of worship. Considering the mother as the Mother Goddess and father as the Father of this world, our home becomes a temple of worship.

These responsibilities need to be explained in some more detail. Since woman , by her very nature, is in a position of power in administering the domain of her activity and had, like her mother, endured enormous mental and physical challenges at her work, her duty is to carry out her three-fold responsibilities , viz. producing progeny to sustain mankind, administering the household, and effecting positive changes in the society. Failure to perform such functions would result in considerable harm. The universe itself will cease to exist if nature stops working. It would have led to the end of this universe and failure of the motive behind creation if only Primal nature had suddenly ceased work immediately after setting the creative apparatus in motion. Similarly, if women fail to perform their functions or take up contrarian activities, it will result in multiple problems like conflicts, societal decline and sordid experiences. There is an adage which exemplifies the invincibility of women. It says that even Lord Brahma can not a stop a woman who is determined on doing something. Whatever good, even a well-intentioned and well-behaved man can ever hope to do to his mother, will pale into insignificance when compared to the severe hardships she had once endured for his sake. What he can do, therefore, are these: Protect those who are grateful to their mothers. Never ever , mentally or physically, take a stand against her wishes, Worship her, and Respect even other women as if they are the incarnations of Mother Goddess Herself. It is one's domestic responsibility to provide for the future generation just as he himself had been given an abode and other necessaries of life by the generation past. On the other hand, if someone intrudes into a space over which he has no right and where he is not invited and feed himself at the expense of others, it would be unrighteous and sinful. A noble human being will carry out his responsibility even if he has to take to begging for that. After all that, in order to keep the wheel of life moving and for the survival of society, he with the approval of his mother gets into married life. When children are born to him as his own alter-bodies, he has to make arrangements to feed, house and clothe each one of them. The one who performs contrarily , instead of discharging his last-mentioned duty adds, in effect, to the trials, tribulations and miseries of this illusory world. In order to carry out his duties satisfactorily, he would do well to remember that he holds no right or claim or desire over his labour or its fruits. If he does not work with such dispassion, he will certainly be frittering away the material wealth he and others related to him had come to possess. A perfect man is one who performs his duties satisfactorily.

Unity is what makes for peace and harmony in the world. Unity between the Cosmic consciousness and the Primal nature sustains this world. Likewise, welfare results from the man-woman unity and misery from their disunity. Likewise is the progress that happens due to the unity between woman and man and the downfall caused due to differences between them. That is why man is considered the *Brahman* and woman the primal nature even at the societal level. Prosperity comes in uninvited when both perform their respective duties harmoniously. But today, human population has increased and such unity between man and woman is missing . It is as if both have lost sense of their assigned duties. They started to believe more in physical prowess. Unity and righteousness declined. Simultaneously want and poverty established its reign all over the world. Earning ones livelihood was simplified to the level of causing injury and harming others. For all the problems that beset the world today like violent riots, revolts and mass struggles, the prime reason is this disunity.

It, therefore, stands proved that the two reasons that cause strife in this world are disunity on the one hand and the instances of man and women pursuing roles contrary to their assigned ones, on the other. Yet another reason which is by no means unimportant is the existence of a certain body of opinions and attempts by people who consider themselves as far-sighted know-alls fit enough to put into practice such opinions. Of course, these worthies do find that unity is the need of the times. The solutions they offer can also be considered as exhaustive . But, regrettably, their ideas suffer from being impracticable due to their pettiness. Because, unity is not something that has to be or is being achieved by either change of attire, food and other habits or speeches made in public meetings. If such activities could bring about unity, then where they are in existence at present, there should be nothing but unity, and wherever they are absent, unity should also be absent. But what we see and experience all around us is just the opposite. And, therefore, to claim that they will usher in unity will be empty and pompous. If only one starts to live in his own home, gets married from among his own folks , looks upon others with compassion and treats them as equals, it is not going to stop unity from emerging. On the contrary, it will certainly help establish unity. But, let us examine the state of affairs with those who champion the cause of unity to the exclusion of the above ideas. 'Madams' who can not even discipline their own children and bring about unity in the households are the ones setting themselves out to teach unity to others. Likewise, the man who brought in nothing into this world when he was born and got himself reared, educated and settled in life through the savings and strivings of his parents and family and who now, instead of doing his bit for the welfare of his family, despite being able to do so, is clamouring for his share in the family estates is the other person who strives to re-establish unity in society. If these are the sort of persons who work for societal harmony and unity, what will happen, except its very opposite? The head of the families, according to their capacities, save something by way of wealth with the intention of keeping their children and , hopefully, the next generations also comfortably placed in life with a little to support themselves with. Is it not against the principle of unity if someone demands his share from that jointly held property? If such discord happens in a place where unity and harmony should prevail, nowhere else in the world is unity going to exist. In fact, when a man's first duty is towards his family of birth and his role should not be above that of a servant there, if he arrogates to himself the position of the all-important personality and tries greedily to gobble up the entire family property, what would be the result? It is just not enough to call them mother-harmers, father-harmers or teacher-harmers. He should in fact be considered as God-harmer for the fact that he squanders , through abandonment of his duties and acts of unrighteousness, wealth earned and kept apart, by dint of unity and with the desire to see them intact for ever, by his parents who take the place of *Shakti* and *Shiva* in his life. If we strive for unity on the basis of what is ethically and morally right for achieving what is our due and in discharge of our responsibilities, disunity will disappear. This sacred formula is by no means a modern discovery. This is a hoary tenet from the remote past. Those who take too much pride in themselves due to modern civilization and hence suffer from distorted vision will not be able to fully understand its full import. Every time, in this world, when disharmony, discord and chaos ruled the roost, great souls who thought in terms of peace and happiness of mankind, have tried to bring misguided souls back into the right path with their advice and counsel. It is those prescriptions that form the basis of religions and sub religions in the world today.

Was it not mentioned that the words and deeds of the present day leaders happen to harm the cause of unity? Therefore to establish harmony and unity, we need to work as follows. If the woman acts according to her nature-given duties with involvement and without occasion for laxity or let-up and with the thought that there is no one else to do it, and, so also, man too strives for the good of his wife and children selflessly and believes that his family's happiness is his own happiness, and thus both man and woman work complementing and supporting each other, the result will be harmonious unity and welfare in the whole world. Doing so would admirably serve the purpose for which one is born in the world.

It is the job of women's organizations to first realize the exact duties and responsibilities of women towards society , propagate those ideals among people and establish the idea that they are the real saviours of society and secure for such views wide acceptance among all. Organizations , like we often witness, are not exactly meant for conducting agitations or holding artistic performances. Before embarking on something new, one should be able to comprehend its likely end results. The attempt for it should be made only when it is certain that through right means right results could be achieved. It should be abandoned, the moment it is anticipated that the results would turn counter-productive and disastrous. That is how wise men behave. Some tend to be enthusiastic in the beginning but subsequently their interest wears off. It should be avoided and all should work in unity till the goal is reached. May be the project would be encountering stumbling blocks and pitfalls initially. But, without getting discouraged one should proceed with the endeavour, thinking of it as one's avowed mission. Like babies with feeble limbs striving beyond their capacities to get up and take little steps, all efforts in the beginning will only be slow and halting. To press on without getting discouraged is to be, finally and certainly, crowned with success and glory. Your efforts should never be wasted on whatever you deem as unnecessary, meaningless or disruptive. Of all things, the most important qualities to be possessed are compassion for others and positive attitude towards all. This attitude will bring success in the personal lives of the participants too.

I offer my prayers for the blessings of the Mother Goddess. May SHE enable women to think of themselves not as separate individuals but as carriers of HER(Mother Goddess) power and not as weaklings but as robust and powerful individuals and perform their just and fair duties.. May they, each one of whom being a minor incarnation of the Mother Goddess Herself, reach positions of all round greatness and glory in their strivings.

(Ends)

CHAPTER THREE

Compassion towards living Beings

(JEEVA KAARUNYA NIROOPANAM)

Paying heed to a particularly relevant Sanskrit saying which says that, of all the teachers, the foremost is this world itself, we shall start this discussion by examining the physical Nature around us first. There are, of course, differences between herbivorous and carnivorous animals in the matter of their appearance and character. The carnivores are distinguished by four sharp and strong teeth. Man too has somewhat similar teeth, leading one to assume that man too is created as a carnivore. Many creatures are out there in the world meant to be used by man as his food. Fish, meat and egg form useful items of food, in that they are tasty, stamina-improving and, forming part of medicinal preparations, and possessing of healing properties too. Innumerable animals get slaughtered in acts such as witchcraft and in rituals connected with propitiating minor gods or demigods, appeasing ghosts, exorcising evil spirits, making offerings to departed souls, worshipping *Shakti* in certain ways, conducting *Yaagas* (sacrifices) , that too by *Brahmins*, and the like. Such large-scale violence perpetrated against several species of animal life, though indeed avoidable, are done knowingly. But nobody has ever been taken to task for such acts in the past. Nor is it happening today. It is as if nobody cares.

Just think of it. If man were to stop all such heinous practices all of a sudden, will he get labeled as non-violent ? No, never. Because, even those, who proclaim that they commit no violence because they eat only vegetables that have no life in them, do not stay away from products like milk and ghee which are categorized as vegetarian stuff by them for their own convenience but are actually very similar to meat . Therefore, if milk can be consumed, meat can also be taken. Some are of the view that non-veg food makes one cruel minded. But it can not be true. How much of meat is the cobra eating to make it so unkind? It is also not correct to say that trees and plants are lifeless and hence they suffer no pain. Because, science says otherwise. According to science, they can feel pain and get affected by intoxicating liquids. So, immovables like trees, plants and grains are as much alive as the movables. That in effect means that even a vegetarian is in some way harming life. So also, numerous lives such as of frogs, ants, worms etc are lost through activities like agricultural operations, travelling, sweeping of the yards, chopping , cooking, walking , lying down to sleep etc. Drinking, eating, breathing and even diarrhea cause loss of lives of minute living organisms such as microbes . No religion or follower of a particular faith has ever remained immune from some connection with killing, because somewhere on the way he would have permitted, abetted or actively participated in it. Instances are there of people of renown who have given up non-veg foods once returning to non-vegetarian stuff again on the advice of knowledgeable people like sages and ascetics. On the other hand we find even some respectable ladies advocating meat eating on the plea that entering the state of *Samaadhi* (the final state of liberation while leaving this earth for yogis) for a recluse requires a minimum of physical stamina, on his part, which meat alone can give and those that oppose this are sinners.

What more is required by way of evidence, heard, experienced or reasoned, either for the present or for the future, to support the cause of non-veg food. Taking a look at the animal life around us, one would see that the frog eats the fly, the snake eats the frog, the wild pig eats the snake, the tiger eats the pig, the lizard eats the spider, the big fish eats the small fish etc.

So, whether on the land or in water or space, the weak is food for the strong. We are also hearing about vines that entwine and plants that entrap animal life that unwittingly gets close to them, devour them and expel only the hard parts like the bones, that exist in different parts of the world. The world seems like it is so designed by god himself as to encourage the predator. On the one side, there is this creature with the right instinct to detect its prey, enough strength to overpower the victim and the required brutishness to kill and make a meal of it. On the other side is the victim engulfed in boundless terror and pain so weak of limb as to fall an easy prey to the marauder. Such contrasting pairs are numerous to find. What is strange is that they are all made to live in close proximity with each other. Pondering on this state of affairs, one would wonder if God's original intent itself was to create a world filled with horror, blood and gore, extremes of pain, and plaintive and pitiful cries of terrified victims.

It seems like God and even Nature around are not only not moved by such heart-rending scenes, but even look like enjoying the sickening spectacle. All in all, killing of one by another seems like an inescapable fact of life, taking place all the time, all around. With the result that even sensible people would think of any attempt to stop such happenings as an exercise in futility.

Except in an enterprise which has a fair chance of success, one can neither talk to another , nor even contemplate, in favor of something that has zero possibility of success . A person advocating non-violence should be totally and completely non-violent himself. There are no such persons around. If someone with a violent attitude speaks, nobody is going to give his words any more meaning than that of an eccentric. As such there is no one in the world who can say that violence should be shunned. But anyone is free to support violence.

This makes one wonder if this universe itself was created to enable violence to play itself out on. All the same, it is also true that even the most determined effort by a whole lot of people can never hope to make this world entirely devoid of all kinds of life-forms even for a second. Even in the absence of killing, death happens regularly and without fail to all that is born. It is, therefore, to be inferred that the creation of this world had nothing much to do with the perpetuation of a violent order in society. In fact, if one can practically remain without breathing, eating , drinking or speaking for a small interval of time, one can at least hope to contribute towards non-violence to that extent. All those who are not children are capable of that much. As such, to be non-violent is easier than to be violent. Man possesses the awareness and power to kill and eat cattle such as goats and bulls. And, inexplicably, the nature keeps the cattle so weak as to be easily overpowered by man, in spite of them being in terrible terror and pain during the process. This could lead one to think that such animals exist as one more item of food for man. In that case, the question arises as to why man himself should not be considered as natural food for wild animals like lions because given an opportunity those animals too kill humans for their food. Such a question appears more meaningful in the light of the fact that animals , unlike men who need to have such things as knives, stove, fire etc to prepare their non-veg food, do not need to possess special implements or tools or spices/ condiments to make a meal of man. Besides, man gets used to meat preparations only gradually, after overcoming the initial aversion he feels towards it. Can one, therefore, conclude that man is created as a natural food to lions etc as are cattle to man.

Consider , for a moment, the case of a steadfast advocate of and believer in violence who sets forth violence to make a tour of the world. Wherever violence chooses to visit, it finds people screaming and scooting in all directions in mortal fear. It finds none to even stand his ground, let alone according a reception to violence. Crestfallen, violence chooses to return and vent its frustration on the man who sent it on the tour. It says: 'You are the only person who supports me in the world. Receive me'. But the man , noticing violence heading for him, develops cold feet . He cries out to non-violence: ' Do not come to me. Please leave me alone'. He takes to his heels, all the while thinking of how to get rid of violence itself. Violence tries to stop him by quoting the very words he uttered in support of it earlier. But he continues his run, even as he hears violence speak, away from it . He was in fact heading towards non-violence. To be able to support violence, one should be able to accept/welcome violence himself. There is absolutely no such person in this world. The fact of the matter is that nobody has the right to advocate violence, while everyone has the right to demand non-violence.

Likewise, the champion of non-violence sent non-violence out on a world tour. It received rousing welcome everywhere and from every man it came across. Homes and streets were found decorated. People bathed and dressed themselves in new clothes and received non-violence with lighted lamps, shower of flowers, ululations, beating of drums and playing of musical instruments. They raised slogans: 'May non-violence stay, May it live long. 'Nobody wanted to send it back. Every one, instead, wanted non-violence to remain with him or her. Watching all this, its master was in tears, even as he went and embraced it. It means that everyone in this world desires non-violence only.

Let us now discuss what herbivores and carnivores are really like and what kind of experiences they deserve to go through. Carnivores like the lion, leopard etc are considered wild and herbivores like cow, sheep, deer etc are considered mild.. The lions naturally want the raw flesh of other animals for food. But it gets it rarely and, that too, with great difficulty. As far as we are concerned meat is something we get used to with effort and is not easily got. Man alone is aware that all creatures go through pain just like him. Wild animals, therefore, are not to be blamed in the least. But man alone is the monster with all the evil in him. If the lion, that looks fair in comparison with man, is to be accorded the adjective ' cruel', man is doubly so and should be called 'cruel,cruel'.. Wild animals wait for their prey for long hours and even days for their food and, once they get it, they make do with whatever they get and that too by finishing it off quickly. Man, on the other hand, gets his prey through an act of purchase , use of force or even stealing and then keeps it for a time to derive the maximum benefits out of it by starving it and making it work as a beast of burden before killing it. Naturally man has got to be considered as not just 'doubly cruel', but as ' terribly cruel'. Another fact is that one animal never encourages another animal to kill. But man does even that and encourages even a non-violent soul to turn violent. And, therefore, man is not just 'terribly cruel', but a hundred times so. If we use the logic man uses to kill a mild animal and also a wild animal rather mercilessly , then he, who is a lot more cruel than the wild animal itself, deserves not just death but a slow and painful death. And in that case, if someone uses his own justification to torment him in whatever way he fancies, no one can fault that person.

There is a view like this: "Just because the act of drinking milk causes the elimination of numerous micro organisms, can we give up drinking milk? Assuming we do, can we stop breathing too, just because it too causes such deaths? Complete non-violence is absolutely impossible to achieve. One can only hope to resolve not to resort to violence wilfully and without sufficient reason ". This view does not appear to be correct. Because, one acts wilfully only when there is a reason behind it. There is even an adage to the effect that even a fool does not act without a purpose.

Suppose a man sitting atop a tree and carrying a loaded gun sights a tiger down below and thinks, 'This tiger is going to kill me, but I want to live for many more years' and he shoots the tiger. In this, 'Will kill me' and ' want to live for many years' are the reasons. The act of killing is deliberate. In case I want to eat goat's meat, I either kill it myself or get it killed by somebody else. Here, the desire to eat meat is the reason. The decision to kill is deliberate. There are instances of children catching small creatures and cutting them open. What could be the reason for that? May be it is due to their inquisitiveness and irresistible urge, like that of the scientist, to see what is inside the creature. Here, the desire to know is the cause. Cutting the creature into pieces is wilful. Wilfulness of children is stronger. When a judge hands out a punishment to an offender, offence constitutes the cause. Meting out the punishment is deliberate. Likewise, when lack of evidence leads to the alleged offender's exoneration, the lack of evidence is the reason for the exoneration that is intentional. Simply stated, it is obvious that there should be some sufficiently strong cause if violence is to make its appearance anywhere. Even a man whose intention is not to cause any harm to living beings in fact unwittingly harms some life or other when he breathes, walks etc. But it would not be as sinful as when an animal is first reared like a child and then slaughtered for food. Neither a threat from the animal to the owner's life, nor an intention to kill for similar reasons, nor wilfulness exist here. People normally tend to lessen the severity of such killings by drawing comparisons with the unpredictability of deaths caused by accidents like the falling of a tree. There is no way of stopping this violence. Hence the statement that one should not kill wilfully and without a reason is a hollow one. The intention of those who make such statements is that violence in all forms should be allowed a free run.

That even plants have life and vegetarians too are guilty of violence is what is going to be discussed below. Some people might think that our forebears were not aware that plants were very much alive like the rest of us. But the fact is that we knew it for a fact from the earliest times. In fact, we have been talking of mobile and immobile life from time immemorial. The western scholars are now only discovering it. Therefore, no one would argue that plants are life less and vegetarians are totally non-violent. It is only that their kind of violence ranks a few notches below total violence and a few rungs above total non-violence.

All living beings fall under the following categories. 1) those that possess only the sense of touch (grass, plants),2) that have only the sense of touch and taste, 3) that have only the sense of touch, taste and smell (corals, ants , worms), 4) that have only the four senses viz. touch, taste, smell and sight (dragonfly, beetle), 5) that have all the five senses of touch, taste, smell, sight, and hearing(Human beings and wildlife). But there is a clear difference between man and animal life. While man's concerns are not about this material world alone, but about the world we inhabit after death or rather an after-life too, animals are concerned with just this world only. When it comes to plant life , sensibilities of pain and pleasure would have become a lot reduced and subdued. Even a man endowed with all the five faculties of perception and the knowledge of the self loses it all in deep sleep. But still he does retain certain faculties in that state too. While he is in sleep, if you call out to him, he at first does not respond; and when called again, he perhaps responds incoherently and on persisting with the calling he comes to his full senses and responds accordingly. In the process, he had passed through three stages which can be classified as no-response, partial response and full response states. Plants and trees, perhaps, occupy a zone somewhat akin to that between no-response and partial response states . In the case of worms and scorpions, when they are cut into two pieces, both parts wriggle about and show signs of life. But with man and large-sized animals, the part with the heart in it alone moves and the other is motionless. Under the influence of anesthesia, man loses all senses, both normal and special. Plants and trees might also be occupying a similar state in which their ability to feel pain and pleasure is at a very reduced level. If consciousness that is capable of shining prior to and subsequent to the application of anaesthetic, remains dormant to make the patient painless during its application, then it is but natural that trees, that have no such capacities to begin with, are with blunted sensibilities. If some plants are exhibiting sudden signs of life when handled, it must be similar to the rare movements noticed on occasion in even dead bodies. There are plants that fold up, and plants that 'weep', when touched by humans. Such examples are many of plants that show clear signs of being disturbed when handled. But they do not show signs of pain, as such. When life evolves from the immobile to the mobile stage, the graph of this ability to perceive pain too climbs up.

Violence has got two evil attributes about it. One is that it inflicts pain on its victim. The second is that it impedes and delays the escape route of the victim. Pain is the most significant factor when beings capable of movement are considered. However, the delay part of it is applicable equally to beings capable of movement as well as not. But people in general are most concerned about pain and least about the interruption caused to their journeys. All people, including the young and old, tend to travel to a place where they are assured of some future gain, good food, friendly people and pleasant environs. Midway through the journey, news comes that on the way ahead of them a tiger had killed two persons in a forested stretch. Certainly, these people will stop there unmindful of all the nice things they had planned to enjoy at the destination. A person under going amputation of one of his limbs has himself chosen to submit himself to anaesthesia and all the privations and inconveniences associated with such a procedure rather than opting for pain and possible death. From all this it becomes obvious that people prefer delay, loss and losing of consciousness etc to death and pain.

Like a ball of wax would contain tiny particles of metals of different grades, every soul takes up a physical form or body in accordance with its innate quality kept preserved in the Moola prakriti or primal nature during the state of Pralaya[1]. In the Pralaya state , all life retain their respective signatures of the stages they have reached in their journeys towards the goal of ultimate Liberation, as part of a sort of evolutionary process. When creation ultimately happens, each form of life breaks out of its respective shell in a form corresponding to the stage it reached in this prolonged evolutionary process, which would have involved being born again and again in a million lives, not necessarily in the same species all the time, marked as they were by uncertainties like episodes of progress as well as that of regression. What unites them all is that they are all engaged in a journey to a common destination, namely, God-realisation.

This journey of the soul gets interrupted when a creature gets suddenly bumped off. It has to take a rebirth and start all over again from the beginning of the evolutionary stage it was not allowed to complete. This means delay. Inflicting this kind of break and delay to the journey of a soul is itself considered as one form of extreme violence by saintly souls. They have tried to stop this also. They held that any creature, ranging from that possessing a single sense through that possessing all the five senses, should not be submitted to any kind of violence and just avoiding killing of a few would not amount to total non-violence. That is why great men declared: 'Non-violence is the highest form of *Dharma*' (*Ahimsa paramo dharma*:).

Now let us examine the case of those who take only vegetarian food. According to western scholars, plants have life but they possess only the sense of touch. Therefore vegetarians kill only this kind of life. They don't need to kill all the other four forms of life occupying positions above plants. This in itself is a great achievement. But those who pride themselves as being non-violent should quickly try to cover all the five groups of living beings. Among them, vegetarians are those who crossed three, four levels. Therefore vegetarians commit the least violence. One obvious question would be about the next level for them. When they realize that even in their kind of food, violence is involved and decide to abjure violence totally, they may do as follows. They can for a beginning try eating fallen leaves and fruits. But it too has an element of violence in it. If they think of living on just plain water, it too is violent in some way. So they start subsisting on just air, the least violent of the options available. In this, they are said to have reached the stage of a *YOGI*. Since even eating air is not entirely non-violent, they strive hard to reach the stage of breathlessness while being alive. This is the much-acclaimed state of liberation or self-realisation or *Samaadhi*. This is a state where that person neither suffers nor inflicts pain and it is the state acclaimed by the progenitors of all religious orders alike. And it is in that state that one had attained the stage of absolute non-violence. This was the kind of non-violence advocated and practiced by our forebears. It is therefore important for us to ignore the voice of the men at large which emphasizes on the futility of seeking after a state of total non-violence because, according to them, whatever way one chooses to live, one is committing some form of violence or other, however minor it might be. Instead, we should consider it our duty to seek to become non-violent through the path described above.

That the kind of food one takes influences one's character is the considered view of many a great man. Swami Vivekananda has himself spoken to the effect that only food that serves to purify the mind should be consumed and the consequence of flouting this rule can be witnessed in a zoo.

What is the effect of non-veg food on the intellect? The truth about it can only be had from the history of great men. In support of this contention, one could quote a number of scholars. Some opined that meat did not contribute to intellectual development, some others said vegetarian food was in agreement with the nature around us, etc, etc. Some of the notable people who held such views included The *Budha, Pythagoras, Newton, St. Peter, St. Mathew* etc.

Certain western medical men hold the view that non -vegetarian food even invites certain ailments. Meat is believed to increase the level of uric acid in blood and cause arthritis, headache, fits, asthma, depression, nervous disorders, diabetes etc. Even it is found that meat intake has increased the incidence of cancer in Great Britain and adoption of veg food like wheat in its place has reduced its incidence.

Canines/incisors of men and carnivores are not similar except in color. Man does not use his teeth as much as an animal does. Molars of humans and animals are very different from each other. But there are similarities between some of the other teeth and digestive systems of humans and apes. So, classifying man as a carnivore is against observed facts. For carnivores, the small intestines are of reduced length. They are about three times as long as their middle body parts. The large intestines happen to be soft. Absorption of nutrients and expulsion of waste take place rather quickly. But, man's small intestines, in comparison, are twelve times as long as their middles and the large intestines are like a bag. And food remains for a longer period there. But meat is a food that does not take long to absorb. Naturally, meat has to be considered as not that fit for the human digestive system. Not only that, meat is said to contribute to incidence of diseases in the case of humans. These observations have been proven to be correct by researchers. Therefore, the stand that humans are natural non-vegetarians is baseless.

Another fact worth taking note of is that life spans are generally long when compared to the time it takes for death to happen, which is usually short. Not only that, nature sees to it that living beings are provided with the right kind of environment to survive and even flourish. Naturally, nature has to be considered as preferring survival or existence more than extinction.

On the basis of the fact that certain beasts and even plants are meat-eaters, to assume that we too can merrily go about consuming meat is not exactly in order. The matter about natural carnivores was discussed. So this argument can apply to those monsters. Natural vegetarians are found both among plant life and animal life. So let the argument that we are natural vegetarians rest with us. It is said that the human body is the noblest of its kind. Lesser beings are with dull intellects. The lesser creatures are created out of *tamasic guna(the dark quality)* . Even Swami Vivekananda has said that beasts are incapable of thoughts of a superior nature. He had also opined that the man and the animals are not far apart from each other when it comes to one's ability to control the emotions, with man a wee bit above that of animals. We have not much control over our minds. That control has to be acquired. From the words of great men it is apparent that the tendency to follow the path set by nature blindly is peculiar to beasts. Any stupid person would be capable of such feats. But, the people who reached positions of renown in public life are the ones who had overcome such easy tendencies with stoic determination. Are we not able to distinguish between mother, sister, wife and an unrelated lady according to established norms? Are we not capable of keeping our minds under control with regard to them? We are also witnessing the travails of those who violate such norms. But such discipline is not seen among animals. It is, therefore, obvious that it is in the nature of man to fight the wayward tendencies of the mind and it is for him to stick to such discipline in life.

Non-violence and Religion.

Since the principle of non-violence finds place in religious doctrines too, it would be in order to take a peek into it.

Hinduism:

There is no need to enquire deeply into what this religion says. It is well known that all the seers and sages of this faith have denounced violence from very early times in strong terms. Non-vegetarian food too is strictly prohibited.

' Hell for the violent and Heaven for the non-violent'

The famed Tamil work *Tirukural* says: ' One who refused to kill the leopard would be worshipped by all'. *(Authors note:* More material has to be added*)*

Jainism:

This religion came into existence in 490 BC. It was established by Sri Vardhamana Mahavira, the son of the king of Vaishali. Its main principles consist of cultivation of habits like Purity etc. How much this religion had decried violence is evident from the practices Jains follow today. They cover up their faces with a net to prevent ingress of tiny critters while breathing lest it should result in their death . Its followers even go to the extent of filtering water before drinking, and sweeping the ground they plan to walk on lest their activities should cause harm to even very tiny creatures. They do not eat after lighting the lamp in the evenings lest some insects get attracted by light and get killed. From all this, it is evident that Jainism never permitted killing of living beings or meat-eating.

Budhism:

This religion was established by Sri *Budha,* the most compassionate. This is very similar to Hinduism and is now prevalent in Japan, China etc. This religion does not believe in a particular God as such. One of its tenets is that what one reaps today is the result of the *karma* (activity) he once sowed. The *Budha* is considered an incarnation of God. The *Budha* himself practiced non-injury to other beings scrupulously while firmly placing this dictum as the prominent tenet of his religion. Under the influence of his rational thoughts and his capacity to put forth arguments in favour of non-injury to living beings , many were the sovereigns who renounced animal sacrifices which were so popular those days and even banned slaughter of animals totally. King Ashoka was one among them. King Asoka's story of sudden conversion from war and bloodshed to total non-violence on his becoming a Budhist is too well known to narrate again. He even established a clinic to treat diseased and injured animals. This religion too prohibits meat-eating.

Christianity.

Its followers are tops, in the matter of civilization, power and good repute. Its founder Jesus Christ was extremely compassionate and devoted to God. One of the tenets of its celebrated Ten Commandments forming its basis forbids people from causing any kind of injury to other living beings. According to its scripture namely The Bible, God after creating Adam and Eve bids them to make use of plants and nut-bearing trees for their food. He never prescribed meat as food. Elsewhere Jesus exclaims to God that he had never in life eaten meat in any form and God in turn is said to have blessed Him. Again, there is the story of his making two persons by name Peter and Andrew whom he met fishing on a certain coast to give up the habit and who later became his devoted followers. Instances such as the above advocating vegetarian food and denouncing eating of meat etc are many in its lore. There is clear evidence that Christ had never ever polluted himself with the least violence or meat-eating. His chief disciples like St. Peter, St. John and St. Mathew too have only followed him in his footsteps. Many scholars and historians of Christianity too testify to this fact. Any information to the contrary recorded anywhere should be due to the handiwork of evil interpreters, according to them. It is also said that Christians did not practice violence or eating of meat down till 1692 AD, after which date the practice of meat- eating somehow found its way into this faith and in order to discuss this matter there was even a meeting of nearly 200 delegates consisting of disciples and emperors drawn from different parts of the world in Constantinople. The meeting resolved to slap severe punishments like expulsion from churches on priests and excommunication from religion on householders for violations of its avowed principle of non-injury to living beings and vegetarianism.

This directive is said to be observed strictly in eastern churches while western churches flout the rule so widely and with impunity that the leaders of the faith are helpless in countering it. There is no use discussing such violation of rules, but what is certain is the fact that this religion too forbids meat-eating.

(ends)

CHAPTER FOUR

Ancient Malayalam

(Prachina Malayalam)

Introduction

Most landlords with large landholdings in this land of *Malayalam*[1] happen to be *Brahmins*[2] carrying the' *Malayali*' (*having to do with Malayalam*) tag. It is also true that a considerable number of people consider these *Brahmins* nobler and more deserving of respect reserved for gurus[3] (*masters who guide others in matters, material and spiritual*) than most others. To justify this unique social position they enjoy, the following two reasons are cited by them.

1.That *Parashurama*[4] had in the remote past forced the sea to recede and yield this land and the new land thus created was gifted by him to them whom he brought in from outside *Kerala*.

2.That theirs is the foremost and noblest of all castes that exist, which qualifies them to hold the position of masters and priests of all the Hindus[5].

What is sought to be established by this work , on the basis of ancient documents, surviving traditions, established practices and by acceptable-to-all reasoning, is that the above claims are baseless. And that this land really belonged to the *Nairs*[6] of this land, who happened to be *Dravidians*[7] of noble birth and owners of vast estates of land

and who by reason of their truthfulness and righteousness came to be cheated and dispossessed of their wealth and prominence by a bunch of *Brahmins* , evil-minded and displaced, who arrived here after having been driven out of their original places. And further that the *Nairs*, riven as they were by internal dissentions, consequently came to occupy lowly positions in the society.

With this aim in view, it is going to be proved that 1)*Brahmins* enjoy no birthright to this land, 2) they are not superior to others in any way and 3) If anything, only *Nairs* can rightfully claim the sort of birthright and position of nobility that the priestly class enjoys.

Of the above three, the first one will be achieved by demonstrating the fallacy of such works as *Sahyadrikhandam*, *Keralamahatmyam*, *Keralolpathi*'s, *Keralavakashakramam* etc because the *brahmini*cal claims are solely and totally based on these works. The other two objectives could be achieved by means of relevant reasoning and by expounding other facts and experiences.

The claim that the *Brahmins* have got a birthright to this land could be demolished in two ways, namely, by reasoning in a general way and by making use of some other specific inputs. The general repudiation , by focusing on the often mutually contradictory and self-negating nature of the contents of the works relied upon like *Sahyadrikhandam*, which prove their unreliability, is discussed in this introductory part itself. The special rebuttal meant to be achieved by dissecting the contents further and proving them to be going counter to established facts, reasonableness and justice will be dealt with in chapters one through four.

General Rebuttal

What follows is an analysis of the differing versions of the *Parashurama* legend itself as found in the texts that support the claim.

a. In the first chapter of the first part of *Sahyadrikhandam* which forms part of '*Skanda puranam*', the story goes like this. *Parashurama* traverses the length and breadth of '*Bharat*' twenty one times and destroys *Kshatriyas*[8] and gifts the land he conquered, as enjoined upon him, to *Brahmins*. He creates a new land next. Its boundaries are *Vaitarani*river in the north, *Subrahmanya* in the south, *Sahyadri* mountains in the east and the high seas in the west. It is 100 by 3 yojanas[9] in extent. *Parashurama* lived on a mountain in this land. Finding that the local *Brahmins* were not cooperating with him in the performance of rituals, he converts fisherfolk into *Brahmins* by breaking off their fishing lines and making sacred threads of them . He made them wear the sacred threads and bestowed *brahminhood* on them. They were settled down in a place called '*Chaturangam*' and were divided into fourteen sub sects or *Gothras*. While taking leave of them, he makes a promise. That he would appear before them whenever they wished so. But, just to check how true the promise is, and without sufficient reason, they stupidly wished for his appearance. Incensed by the act, he curses them that they would all become evil quacks, reprehensible and poverty-stricken, and earn their bread doing menial jobs.
b. The same text deals with the same story in its sixth chapter in a different way. In '*Vaamana*[10]' incarnation, Lord *Vishnu* gifts " *Bali*'s" land to sage *Kasyapa* who in turn gifts it to *Dravidas, Gowdas, the Aryavarta*scholars

etc. In *'Treta yuga', Kartaveeryarjuna* and his descendents managed to occupy the land by foul means. As a result of the prayers of *Kasyapa, Lord Vishnu*, incarnates as the son of *Jamadagni* and *Renuka*. He takes the name, *Parashurama*. From Lord *Shiva*, he gets his battle-axe, with which he went about annihilating the *Kshatriyas*, by going round and battling them, not just once or twice but twenty one times over. After securing the land and handing it over to *Kasyapa*, he went up the *Sahya* mountains and sat there lost in thoughts. Sage *Narada* appeared before him and learning that he was worried about the fact that he was now left with no land to stay on, advised him to make the sea recede. He acts accordingly and creates a new land by sending an arrow across the sea. *Banavalli* is the name of the town that came up where the arrow landed. This land named Rama kshetra included the seven *Konkanas* called *Thulangam, Saurashtra, Konkan, Karahatam, Karnatak and Karbaram*. Here, at the place, *Gokarna*, *Shiva* resides. Ten *yojanas* north, at *Saptakoteeswaram, Parashurama* seated himself. Then, he brought in *Brahmins* from outside and settled them there. Like in the earlier story, his promise , its testing and the curse follow in that order. Only this time, as a consequence of the curse, they are to turn ill-informed, haughty, and hateful. They would live by breaking rules and serving *kshatriyas* and would reach such a lowly position as to beg for alms before *Sudras*. They would be performers of evil rituals and sellers of boons.. They would happen to go without children when moneyed and have many children when in penury. But this curse becomes inoperative in the *Kali Yuga*[11], the age of the evil, only.

c. The seventh chapter of the same book says that *Parashurama* had performed an *Aswamedha Yajna* and gifted this land to the chief priest of this *yajna*, namely, Kasyapa. But the officiating priests of the event immediately ask *Parashurama* to go some place else, as by then, the land belonged to them. So he climbs up the *Sahya* mountain, prays to the sea God, *Varuna*, on whose advice he throws his axe across the sea. The sea withdraws beyond the trajectory of the weapon. The land so created extended from *Kanyakumari* to *Nasikathrayambakam*. It contained the seven regions mentioned above. For *Brahmins*, he converted fishermen by making them wear sacred threads made of their own broken fishing lines. They too get cursed following the same sequence of events as described above. But this time it differed in one respect , in that , as eaters of forbidden food and wearers of fragmented clothes, they would, however, one day come to be lauded in the land called '*Asiprastavani staanam*'. Subsequently, King *Mayooravarman*, during his reign, finding the deplorable state of the *Brahmins* in the land, brings in *Brahmins* from '*Ahichatra*' and settles them down in an area divided into 32 villages. As *Kali*'s reign grew stronger, the king relinquished his kingship and went away. At this, they too headed back to *Ahichatra*, but finding that they were unwelcome there, settled down outside the place. Long years after, *Chandraangada*brought them back to the same villages they left once, but with a stipulation that they would sport a tuft of hair in the front part of their scalps as a mark of identification.

d. The story, according to the fourth chapter of the next work namely '*Kerala mahatmyam*' goes thus. After annihilating *Kshatriyas* 21 times over, *Parashurama* did several propitiatory rites meant for absolution from the sin of his acts and finally on the advice of the sages made the ultimate sacrifice of gifting the land to the *Brahmins*. Once the deed was done, the *Brahmins* resented his presence in the gifted land. So he went to *Kailas* and prayed to Lord *Shiva*. He returned from *Kailas* accompanied by *Shiva*'s son, Lord *Subrahmanya*, and went straight to *Kanyakumari*. There he prayed for a year before Goddess *Vishnumaya* made manifest there by *Subrahmanya* . Due to *Shiva*'s grace, the goddess appears before him and grants him his wish. Consequent to that *Varuna* advises him to hurl his axe away with his left hand into the sea. On doing so, the sea recedes beyond the area covered by its flight. The extent of the land so created was 100 by 10 *yojanas*.

e. Now, let us examine what yet another text namely '*Keralolpathi*' says. According to this work, after fulfilling the purpose of his incarnation viz. elimination of the whole *Kshatriya* class, he needed to expiate his guilt and purify himself of the sin of killing so many lives. He therefore prayed to Mother Earth at *Gokarna* and created a new land measuring 160 *kaatams*, where he consecrated 108 *Shiva* temples. Finding that it did not purify him completely, he brought in *Brahmins* from far and settled them down there. But they ran away because of their fear of the *Nagas* living there. After a while, they were brought back again. Their attire and customs were changed and asked to stay on permanently.

f. In deciding the question of birthright to this land, claimed by them, the matter to be looked into are the following:

1.The reason for creating the *Malayalam* land

2.The modus operandi of such creation.

3.The land's boundaries and extent

4.The reason for the gifting of the land.

1.The summary of what has been told by way of the purpose of creation of land is as follows.

'*Sahyadrikhandam*' itself is full of contradictions when it comes to the purpose. In one chapter, after the destruction of *Kshatriyas* , *Parashurama* is said to have gifted some land. Then *Parashurama* goes about creating another land.

In another section it states that the creation of land happens on the advice of sage '*Narada*'. The purpose is for *Parashurama* to stay on.

In yet another place, it states that creation follows '*Varuna*'s' advice because the priests have objected to his continued presence in the gifted land.

According to *Kerala mahatmyam* , the gifting, as *Parashurama* represents before Lord *Shiva*, is the result of an act of treachery. As such, those who make the creation of land possible are Lords *Shiva*, *Subramania*, *Vishnumaya* and *Varuna*.

2.Now, let us summarise the different acts that resulted in the creation.

Sahyadrikhandam' is silent about the method of creation when it describes the event first. In its subsequent narrations, at one place, it is the dispatch of an arrow from the *Sahyadri* across the sea and in another place it is his axe that does the job. In *Kerala mahatmyam*, it is the left-handed hurling of the axe with *Vishnumaya*'s help. In *Keralolpathi*, he is seated near *Gokarna* while creating the land and it is achieved by praying to Lord *Varuna*.

3.The boundaries and extent mentioned in different places too are at variance with one another. In

Sahyadrikhandam, in one place it is 100 by 3 in extent and between Vaitarani and *Subrahmanya*, in another place it is 100 by 5 and includes seven regions and in yet another place it lies between *Kanyakumari* and N*asikathrayambakam,* but includes the 7 regions. In *Kerala mahatmyam*, the area is 100 by 10, boundaries remain unspecified, but *Kanyakumari* looks like included since the action takes place there. In *Keralolpathi* too the boundaries are not mentioned, but the extent is 160 *kaatams.*

4.*Sahyadrikhandam* and *Keralamahatmyam* do not mention about any gifting of the *Malayalam* land.

Keralolpathi says it was done as a rite of absolution from sin incurred by killing *kshatriyas.*

The *Kerala Avakaashakramam*too says it was a rite to rid himself of sin , but only to remove some residual sin.

The descriptions of events in the above books, about the bringing in of *Brahmins*, their going back, and their coming back again are contradictory to each other and lacking in credibility. For example, the fact is that when the *Nakas* who happened to be the original inhabitants of the land and who were warriors challenged the entry of outsiders, the intruders ran away. But in response to their subsequent pleadings some of them were allowed to settle down. But tweaking such facts, they have written things down differently. Making use of the similarity in sounds between '*Nakas*' and the Sanskrit word '*Nagas*' meaning serpents, they misrepresented that the land was infested with snakes and hence they had to leave in the beginning.

In any investigation, when the evidence on hand and the statements of witnesses are at variance and contradictory, it can not be relied on and hence has to be rejected., and when they are agreeable and believable, they will have to be accepted. As such, since the matter dealing with the issue of their birthright in their own texts are contradicting each other, it follows that they do not enjoy any birthright over this land.

However, there could be another view too on this entire issue. On the basis of ground realities and experiences and also in view of the fact that the events narrated follow almost the same pattern all through, it could be argued that the contradictory nature of the material on hand, by way of evidence, should not matter much. In that case, we have to accept that this land was indeed created by *Parashurama* and it was gifted by him to them with all rights, ownership and lordship over it and *Nakas* were meant to only serve them .

What follows, from the next chapter onwards, therefore, is the establishment of the baselessness of the questions inherent in this issue separately.

Chapter 1

Gifting was not at all called for:

The reason cited for the gifting was the removal of the sin incurred by *Parashurama* consequent to the slaughter of *Kshatriyas*.

Kerala mahatmyam says the decision to eliminate the *kshatriyas* was taken by the sages. It was their advice to kill king *Kartaveeryarjuna* and other *kshatriyas* in retribution for the killing of *Parashurama*'s own mother by the king and also with the intent to protect the innocent subjects from the deeds of evil rulers. The saviors of the world are apt to carry out good deeds in the guise of rites of absolution in order to enlighten ordinary mortals who take arrogant pride in their money power, numerical strength and youthfulness. Naturally, *Parashurama*'s can not be considered a sinful act.

Parashurama is said to have sought advice from sages as to how to execute the gifting of land meant for absolving himself of the sin on his part before acting according to their instructions. At the end of the ritual, sage *Viswamitra*, who is the very repository of righteousness, is said to have exclaimed with happiness: ' It is wonderful. What you have done is enough'. After this announcement from the sage, there is no possibility of any sin sticking to him.

Further he is said to have openly declared before the ceremony that he was gifting all the worlds to the *Brahmins* in order to rid himself of all his sins. But *Kerala mahatmyam* says some sin was still left with him. It sounds baseless.

Further, *Parashurama* is no ordinary mortal. One has to take into account his enormous *Jnana*, *yoga* and *tapas*[12]. Someone possessing such spiritual faculties alone would be capable of executing such feats as creating land out of the seas. *Parashurama* is credited with the accomplishment of such feats. A man carrying a baggage of sin , however small it might be, will just not be able to accomplish that.

Ancients[13]'declare that '*Tapas*'(penances) removes all sin on the part of the person who undertakes it. Attainment of the yogic state means obliteration of all sin. In *Bhagavad Gita*, Lord Krishna says : '*Jnana* destroys all sin'. The text, *Soota samhita*, declares: ' Even if one had performed one thousand horse-sacrifices and one hundred killings of *Brahmins*, when he attains *Jnana*, all his sins vanish'. *Kaushitaka Upanishad* says: 'Even the killing of one's own father, mother and foetus does not affect the man with *Jnana*'. *Sruti*[14] declares: 'Action(karma) does not attach itself to a *Yogi* just as the lotus leaf remains unsullied by water'.'*Brahma sutra*' too makes this assertion:' Attainment of *Jnana* is followed by destruction of sin both prior and subsequent'.

Parashurama is one who has got his spiritual initiation from the great sage *Dattatreya* (according to the text *Tripura rahasyam*). He is one who had attained the highest states of *Jnana, Yoga* and *Tapas*. He qualifies himself as a sage of the first order.

Naturally no sin should remain attached to such a lofty soul as *Parashurama*. There was absolutely no need on his part to go through such propitiatory rites such as gifting of vast lands. And therefore the theory that he gifted lands for such a purpose is untenable.

Chapter 2

So also, *Brahmins* were not brought in from outside.

Summary:

In the previous chapter it was proved that there was no sin on the part of Parashuraman and so there was no need for him to gift lands. In this chapter it is going to be proved that he did not bring in *Brahmins* from outside. The arguments in this connection and the resolution of the issue will be dealt with here for the benefit of the readers.

1.Like in other castes, in *Malayali Brahmins* too, we find divisions into sects and subsects nowadays. The works like *Kerala mahatmyam, Kerala Avakashakramam* etc that deal with this subject, attribute these divisions to the act of receiving of gifts and the like. There is no doubt that receiving of gifts form the main reason and all the other reasons came in afterwards. Those who received are considered polluted and those who did not are considered pure even now. Let us examine if such conclusions are justified.

2.If receiving of gifts from *Parashurama* should cause pollution to the recipients, the donor himself should have been polluted in the first place. But it was concluded in the previous chapter itself that he was sinless and hence was not polluted. So, to say that *Brahmins* got polluted on this account is not correct.

3. The recipients should not get tainted if only they are meticulous practitioners of their daily routines and rites. Since it is stated that they were tainted, one has to only assume that they were not rigorous practitioners of their prescribed *karma (routines)*. In this regard, the tainted ones who received and the untainted ones who did not receive the gift out of fear are both in the same league. Naturally they can not be considered as possessors of those noble qualities that their texts say they possessed.

4.If in case tainting occurred not due to their ineligibility to receive but due to *Parashurama*'s own considered decision to that effect, it is highly unlikely that he introduced a new practice, that too, in violation of provisions in *Smritis*and *Srutis*, when he had not employed it in the other gifting rituals performed by him in places outside *Kerala* earlier.

5.Texts declare that *Parashurama* gifted to the eligible ones only. The sign of such eligibility is that it is capable of destroying the sin on the part of both the recipient and the donor. Since in this case, the *Malayali Brahmins* got tainted in the process, it follows that he did not bring any of them from outside *Kerala*.

A note on *brahmini*cal castes, sects, and subsects.

In the *Brahmin* class, castes are eight, sects or sub castes are two and sub sects are twelve. According to the text '*Jaathi nirnayam*', the castes are these:

1.*Samrats(Thambraakals), 2.Aaddyas (Ashtagriha), 3.Vishishta brahmins, 4.Saamanya brahmins, 5.Jaati matras, 6. Saanketikas, 7.Shaapa grastas,8.Paapis or sinners.*

The *Samrats*enjoy four *Parashurama*-given titles which they and their descendents can enjoy for ever and ever. They are *Bhadrasanam, Saarva maanyam, Brahma saamrajyam, and Brahmavarchas.*

2.*Aaddyas*: They are the *Namboodiripads.* Penance, knowledge of Vedas, lordship, and righteousness are the four pursuits ordained upon them by *Parashurama.*

3.*Visishtas*: They are authorized to perform sacrifice called *Agnihotra.* Life of renunciation, getting sacrifices performed by other *Brahmins*, and the work of *Bhatas* are their other duties. Depending on the line of work, they are further classified as *Atithiri(Aahitagni), Chomathiri(Somayaji), Akki thiri(Agnichit), and Bhatathiri*(who perform as Bhattas)

4.*Saamanyas*: Learning of Vedas, *Sanyas* or life of renunciation, witchcraft or practices with *mantra* recital, and tantra of temples form their line of work.

5.*Jaatimatras*: There are four sub sects among them. They, in the decreasing order of their social status, are:

a.*Ashtavaidyas* or those practicing traditional medicine, b. Those who took up weapons at the instance of *Parashurama*, c. Those who took up avocations other than those connected with Vedas due to disease or old age and d. Those who, under influence of desire, anger etc, gave up Vedas and took up other activities. *Ashtavaidyas* are generally called *Nambooris* and specially as *Moos* and *Nambi.* The 3rd and 4th categories go by the name *Nambooris.*

6.*Saanketikas*: These are the ones who, after arrival, ran away due to problems they faced here and came back later with *Parashurama*'s permission. They go by the name *Embran.* Some of them follow *Malayala* traditions; some, traditions from outside *Malayalam*; and some, mixed traditions.

There are six classes among them: *Tiruvalla desi, Tripoonithura desi, Akkaradesi, Ikkaradesi, Karnatakas, and Thoulavas*. The first two were patronized by Kolattiri kings and Tripoonothura kings respectively; the 3rd and 4th by the *Kulasekharar*oyalty; and the 5th and 6th are peripatetic and they travel in the southern parts. These six classes were settled by *Parashurama* in 32 villages. Their duties are: Temple rituals, learning of Vedas, *namaskaara bhakshanam, and parikarmam.*

7.*Shapagrasthar*: They carry the curse of *Parashurama* and other acharyas. They are also called *Nambooris*. But they are supposed to learn things outside of the Vedas (aveda patam). *Anamaskaara bhakshanam*(the opposite of *namaskara bhakshanam*), *Apoojyatvam* (Inegibility to be accorded honours) and *Asahastiti*(may be inability to be seated along with others considered pure and noble) are also part of their lot.

8. *Paapis*: (The name itself mean they are sinners). There are five sub sects among them. They are:

a.Those who accepted the gift, b. *Graamanis* who permitted killing of Perumal, c. The *Panniyoor* villagers who abandoned the *Varaahamurty* deity , d. *Ilayats* who chose to officiate in ceremonies of *sudras*, e. *Nambidis*who killed *Perumal* with permission from *Brahmins*.

Among the five, the first three are graded in the matter of sin and status. The last two suffer from caste differences too.

Besides, those who do things which are classified as sinful in the ancient texts are also termed *Paapis.*

Those belonging to the eight major divisions are all generally called *Nambooris*, in addition to their special names. Some of those in the 5th and 6th divisions are called

Potties. Among them, some with higher status are called *Nambidis* (*pandarathil*). The sixth category go by the name *Embran,* but in some places they are *Potties*. Those in the 7th category are called *Namboori*. The 8th category people address the third category as *Nambooris,* but call all the others with their sub sect names. The matrilineal *Payyanoor* people are called '*Ammaavans*'.

As stated above, some of them are tainted due to gift-receiving and some others due to other later reasons. Naturally, on account of the taint on their parts, they would not have been the ones brought in by *Parashurama*.

Kerala mahatmyam states that they were all pure when brought in. On this basis, as well as due to the fact that those untainted ones are still considered pure, it can be argued that when *Parashurama* brought them in for the first time they were all pure and unsullied and their fall from such purity happened in time due to other reasons.

The above statement does not apply here:

Some who chose to participate in the gifting ceremony got polluted, and those who stayed back remained untainted. It follows from this that the latter escaped tainting by mere staying back. In other words, all of them originally belonged to the same category in terms of their spiritual prowess. Hence all of them have to be considered as ineligible candidates to receive such gifts.

Hence the above statement does not wash.

Receiving gifts does not make one tainted

The sin under discussion is the sin that *Parashurama* incurred by killing *kshatriyas*. It is the same sin that had got transmitted to those who received the gifts. It means *Parashurama* himself was initially polluted. In that case he would have been barred from all holy ceremonies. But all evidence and reasoning points to the contrary. And, hence, there must have been other reasons for their getting polluted. Gift-receiving, certainly, can not be the reason.

Parashurama's decision

The text, *Saankara* smriti, dealing with *Malayala Brahmin* matters has the following to say in its chapter 1, section 2, verses 9 and 10:

"Sri *Parashurama*, the incarnation of Lord *Vishnu*, considers receiving of land as gift in his own land of *Malayalam* as lowly in nature and hence hold the same as demeaning among the duties of *Brahmins*. The *Brahmins* who receive such gifts will be looked down upon by the noble ones. The noble ones will be ashamed of such deeds.(The Sanskrit root of) 'laj' that stands for shame, in time, got corrupted into 'jal'. From Jal comes 'Jalmi' which with further corruption into 'Janmi' stands for land-owner. There is, therefore, a view that it is how receiving of land as gift became a polluting act".

Parashurama would not have taken such a decision:

Parashurama would not have held receiving of land as gift as tainting in nature, only in the *Malayalam* land . He had in fact gifted the whole of Bharata before to the *Brahmins*.

To quote from *Kerala mahatmyam* itself:

Parashurama wiped out the entire *kshatriyas* belonging to the two clans through twenty one expeditions by killing even their successive progenies . After destroying *Karthaveeryarjuna* and others, he by himself looked after the entire conquest in a fair and just manner. He performed obsequies for the killed ones, in their own blood.

Though, he had performed lots of charities before and since, he came to know through sage *Narada* that sage *Viswamitra* desired that he should perform gifting of land too.

He , therefore, in a ceremony of flowers and water, gifted all the land falling within the four seas. *Brahmins* blessed him individually. Then, when he enquired of them if anything more needed to be done, except for *Viswamitra* every one else sat embarrassed. Thereupon, *Viswamitra* asked him to go away to either the sea or the skies as his entire land now stood gifted. Acceding to the demand, after wishing them well, he went to Sri *Kailas*, the abode of Lord *Shiva*, and saluted the Lord. The Lord asked him if he had happened to part with the land through an act of treachery.

It therefore follows that the gifting was effected by the device of cheating by the others in a thoughtless moment of his. As such, it is the the act of gifting that has to be termed as sinful. Even so, according to all evidence and experiences, *Parashurama* is never found to have declared the act as reprehensible or causing of pollution on the part of the recipients in small or large measures. Nor is there any evidence that such pollution, even to this day, exists as an irredeemable feature of their lives.

As for this land, it was never in occupation by anybody else and it never needed to be retrieved by violent means from anyone.

Again quoting significantly from the same text:

' This land of *Kerala* (*Malayalam*) is one that was created by *Parashurama* by his own effort with due help from Lord *Subrahmanya*, where the entire three hundred and thirty million gods including *Brahma, Vishnu and Maheswara* and all the sages shower their blessings repeatedly, where Lord *Kubera*'s treasures exist, and which is heaven-like because of the presence of celestial looking women living therein. Besides, both the donor and the recipients were *Brahmins* of great nobility".

On this basis, anybody has to agree that this particular gifting has to be considered as more correct than and far superior to any other gifting executed from the earliest times down to the present. *Parashurama* is not a mentally unstable personality to misjudge this noble act of his as something bad which would cause harm to his own people. And, therefore, it is incorrect to say that pollution was caused by the receiving of the gift of land.

Prescribed spiritual practices destroy sin accrued on account of gift-taking.

Let us assume for a moment that receiving of gifts brings in sin too. We are going to see that even in that case one can remain untainted.

Saankara Smriti (Chapter 1, section 2, verse 11) states:

"However, when a *brahmin* chooses to subsist on what remains of his income after giving away a sufficient part of it to Fire(*Agni*), the preceptor(*Guru*), Guest (*Atidhi*), kinsmen and sages, no sin accrues to him".

The same text(Chap5, section4, verses 1-5) states:

Only *Brahmins* and not others are authorized to accept gifts in the form of charity. If such charity is not accepted, it will be the end of charity itself. The sin or pollution that befalls that man can be remedied by adopting methods prescribed by sages. It is as follows.

Only a householder who scrupulously performs his religious routines can accept charity. Because his routines destroy the sin that accrues.

The said text describes the routines on performance of which the person shines like *Agni*. Therefore, though gift-taking brings in sin, since it is removable, the sin can not last even for a small period of time. Moreover *Brahmins* and lower castes are in the habit of performing such charitable acts from the past and *Brahmins* themselves receive such charities.

This is particularly true of the *Brahmins* of this area rather than of any place else.

The reason for the taint is certainly not gift-taking. If it is, then it means that the recipients lack the necessary spiritual prowess. *Parashurama* will never bring in such flawed people. Nor did he ever do.

Since routines for absolving oneself of sin that accrued and making one shine like fire are well-established, they have to accept that they were lowly people without such practices. If they accept that the tainting was not caused by charity-acceptance, then they will have to give up the claim to this land at once. And it will be the end of this debate. Or else if they accept that they are people without the required spiritual practices, they will automatically become ineligible for this act of charity.

Saankara Smriti (chap 5, section 4, verse 5) says:

"Only a householder who performs his prescribed duties regularly can accept charity. The man who does not, can not".

Parashurama's opinion was also the same in the matter. *Saankara smriti and Bhargava Smriti*too agree on this point.

While sending for a *Brahmin* during an earlier charity, *Parashurama* instructs his messenger:

"Go, bring quickly a *brahmin* eligible for charity"

While handing the gift, he says;

" I give you ten gifts. Because, are not *Brahmins* worthy of receiving charity?".

A *Parashurama* who was so cautious and scrupulous about such matters would not forget it when he seeks out *Brahmins* for receiving charity. He would never have brought in ineligible ones. If it is that he made an exception to this rule when gifting the *Kerala* land, then one can refer to *Kerala mahatmyam*, chapter 11 etc where it is unambiguously stated that he brought in only noble *Brahmins*.

Based on the above arguments, the requirement of a state of sinlessness to justify the eligibility to receive charity applies equally to everyone from the highest to the lowest of *Brahmins*. It has therefore to be concluded that *Malayali Brahmins* were certainly not brought in by Sri *Parashurama*.

Chapter 3

Parashurama had never gifted his land

According to the texts like *'Jaati nirnayam'*, the entire *Malayali Brahmins* belong to sixty four villages named therein. It is to all of them that *Parashurama* gifted his land. But some of them are said to have got polluted and the rest not. The explanation is that only those that went through the gift-receiving ceremony involving water and flowers and accepted the charity either for themselves or on behalf of others got both lands and the sin and the others who received through proxies received only the land but not the sin. But, then, how is it that some *Brahmins* of these 64 villages remain landless. There is no explanation for that. Since the explanation for the former is unacceptable and that for the latter is absent, one has to conclude that the statement that Parasurma's charity went to all of those villagers is not correct. It can only mean that *Parashurama* never gave anything to any *Brahmin*, whether it was the highest among them or the lowest namely the sinner. Since *Kerala mahatmyam* states emphatically that the gifting covered all without exceptions, all should be in possession of lands. But it is not the case. Therefore the above statement and the general impression among people to that effect are erroneous. If he had indeed left some of them out, then *Parashurama* becomes an unfair person.

As it is said that *Parashurama* had brought in noble *Brahmins* from outside *Kerala* and after some of them went away, he felt bad about it, and in order that others too did not leave, he changed them in such a way that they began to wear a frontal tuft of hair on their heads along with changed attire and were taught a distinctly different articulation of Vedas. If he had taken so much trouble just to keep them from deserting again, it is improbable that he had left some of them without gifts . In fact he should have given the same wealth and status to the ones who did not personally take the gifts as he had given to those who personally received the gifts at the ceremony. Although he professed eternal enmity with the *kshatriyas*, whoever among them surrendered were brought by him and settled down in comfort. To say that such a person had left some of them ,who had come in at his request in the first place and who had no means of survival to begin with here , high and dry is improper. If it was because they were not actually cold-shouldered but they themselves had declined the favour, then why at all did they come here in the first place? If it had happened by some strange mistake, then they would have left this place immediately, without choosing to go through the troublesome transformation he effected in their appearance and practices subsequently.

But if they came in not by invitation but clandestinely and it is because of that they were left out, then, there is no document or public opinion in support of it. Besides, even if they were unauthorized entrants, *Parashurama* who had invited them to come in initially, would not have neglected them, who were prepared to stay back here for ever. Because of this and because they were not even participants in the proxy-gift-receiving that happened, the view that all the sixty four villagers were benefited by gifts does not appear to be in order.

What is obvious here is that these *Brahmins* strongly believe that gift-taking, when it brings in wealth, also brings in sin that never goes away. It is also found that the basis for all ownership and lordship that exist here is the above-mentioned charitable act. Since the titles the highest among them enjoy is obtained from the *Parashurama*'s charity, they should have incurred sin too along with it. But it does not seem to have happened. The highest are the highest even now.

Explanation: Sin accrues only when the act of receiving is done with one's own hands. Some of them have not received with their hands and hence there is no sin on their part.

Rebuttal: It looks like *Parashurama* had out of compassion decided not to pollute the holy *Brahmins* and so the gift was placed at some place else for them to take away and enjoy. But such a man of compassion could have employed the same method in the case of the ones who got tainted also. But he does not seem to have chosen to do that. It only goes to prove that such a method was unacceptable to him and therefore he had never employed it.

It is not known if sin that attaches itself to the recipient is capable of going some place else. In proxy gift-taking, if it is said that the sin either goes back to the donor himself or alternately it remains suspended for some time before it wears itself out in time, it does not stand to reason.

In propitiatory/purificatory gift disbursals, the recipient has to personally accept the gift from the donor. Then only it will have its desired results of absolving the donor of his sin and according the recipient with the ownership of the gift. Ownership can not be claimed by persons who did not personally take part in the formal ceremony. If they have ownership, it must have come about through some other route.

But, even though the unpolluted had not received personally, others had. If the latter's action had turned out to be to the former's benefit, and since the latter did not own any land before, all the lands they got from *Parashurama* should have gone to the former.

Explanation: The gift was received specifically under two separate accounts, one for themselves and the other, for the others. What was obtained for themselves alone would be retained with them as their own.

Rebuttal: In that case, did they receive the sin separately or along with the gift ?. Suppose that the gift came in with sin as part and parcel of it. *Kerala mahatmyam* proclaims that it was so and the sin needed to be removed. The gift giving and receiving is also done for that specific purpose only, when the sin is supposed to pass from the donor to the recipient. For that to happen, the act of receiving should be with one's own hands. Therefore the right over the lands received for one's own use and for the others' use should have been with the persons whose hands it was that received them. Even if they were magnanimous enough to part with what was got by them in others' name at a later date, at least the property received under one's own name should have continued to remain with the actual recipients. It therefore follows that ownership first lay with *Parashurama*, secondly with those who personally received the charity and thirdly with the social high-rankers or the untainted who received it from the tainted. And therefore the untainted can not claim that they received it from *Parashurama*.

Supposing that those who received with their own hands received only the sin and not the lands, then the act of charity can not be considered as the reason for the acquisition of ownership by the untainted ones. It has already been established that they received nothing from *Parashurama*. Therefore *Parashurama*'s charity can also not form the reason. Will anybody be prepared to receive destruction-causing sin alone ? Charity is not about that. How a purificatory gift giving ceremony is to be conducted has been demonstrated by *Parashurama* himself before. Its result is absolution from all sin for the donor and enjoyment of the gift for the recipient. Though what the donor gave away was the gift along with his sin, the aim is that the gift should be enjoyed and the sin should suffer dissolution. Therefore what got transferred was the gift alone and not the sin, which is corroborated by *Parashurama* himself. If someone says that the gift he received did not have any material part to it, it can not be correct.

Now, it is going to be shown that the contention that when the transfer of property happened from the tainted to the non-tainted, the sin alone did not stay with the latter but went back to the tainted is incorrect.

This is how proper gifting is to be done. The donor supposes his sin upon the to-be-given gift and then gives it away with the assumption that the sin is also going with it. If the gift is too large to be held by hand, the supposition happens on the water with flowers in it that symbolically takes the place of the actual gift . The recipient receives the gift with the assumption that he is receiving it along with the donor's sin. This way the sin gets transferred to the recipient. The assumption by the recipient is of such nature that it significantly prevents the return of the sin to the donor again. The sin so received is destroyed by the recipient by means of the power of his penance. As compensation for his act, he rightfully enjoys the gift thereafter.

What is getting transferred through hands is not sin alone but the material gift also and therefore for the two to exist apart at two different places is impossible.

Explanation: Since those who have received the gift with their hands happen to retain a portion of it as their own, the sin pertaining to the other portion given away will also sit with them.

Rebuttal: In that case where will that part of the sin go ? If it can also sit with their share of the gift, why at all did they give away the corresponding material part of the gift?

Further, under the circumstances, two things remain inexplicable. It was in the powers of the untainted lot to rid the tainted people, who had undergone a great sacrifice by willingly accepting even the sin that should have rightly gone to the untainted ones, by performing rituals meant for the purpose. But they do not seem to have done that for ages and they have only let the poor tainted ones remain tainted all this while. Secondly, the tainted people themselves could have demanded rightfully of the untainted ones the same thing. But they too have not done that. Instead they seem to have chosen to, without protest, remain as tainted and consequently occupy a lower position in the social order than the untainted ones. This state of affairs could have come about under one possibility only. That the ones who have received the gift with their own hands have not done so with the due assumption that they were receiving the sin too on behalf of those who stood away from the ceremony while receiving the share of gifts due to those who stayed away.

Explanation: This is true of only this gifting. Therefore it is not likely that remedies are mentioned in the Vedas, *Srutis* etc. That is why it remains unresolved and not because they are unwilling.

Rebuttal: The instance of the gift and its associated sin existing separately in two different places is unheard of. May be because of that, the remedy is not prescribed.

Explanation: Those who received have also accepted the sin due to the others(non-participants). That is how the untainted received their properties.

Rebuttal: Then, it should have been the case with all. But here some among the untainted are earning their livelihood as mere tenants under landlords. Therefore that contention can not be true.

Explanation: Proxy-gift-acceptance took place only in respect of some, not all.

Rebuttal: There is no justification for that. According to *Kerala mahatmyam, Parashurama* exclaims: ' Land was gifted by me to all the gothras (sects) of *Brahmins*'. Such a fair minded person would not have done an unfair job like that.

Explanation: In this particular gifting alone, he adopted such a partisan approach.

Rebuttal: This goes against the stand that *Parashurama* had gifted the entire *Kerala* to all the sixty four villagers.

Now, let us examine the reason for their non-participation . Was it because they suspected something bad or *Parashurama* had refused to give them gifts?

If it was due to such suspicion, then they would not have come over here and decided to stay put here like refugees. Besides the eligible ones need not have such fears. If they are fearful, then they become ineligible and their ownership turns out to be not due to *Parashurama*'s charity. But certain sections of *Kerala mahatmyam* discounts such a possibility. They also say that the *Aaddya*(*Ashtagriha*) *Brahmins* owe their origin to the same parents. In that case they must belong to the same *gothra*(sect). But marriage within the same gothra is not permitted . Since marriages do happen among them it has to be inferred that they belong to different gothras.

Parashurama has not gifted lands to even the tainted ones.

Why at all did *Parashurama* secure, with much effort, this land from the sea. It can not certainly be for earning absolution from sin, because the aim of ridding himself of all kinds of sin he carried with him had been already achieved by the first two giftings he performed, one by giving away all the lands and the other called '*Shodasa*' that consisted of sixteen different kinds of gifts. Because even the dull-headed will not act except with a purpose, when we examine to find *Parashurama*'s exact intent for creating new land from the sea, we would come to the conclusion, based on the foregoing discussion, that it was only for him to settle down. There was absolutely no need for him to do any fresh gifting.

Even if we assume that he had stayed in the new land for a while and then went away after handing the land over to the *Brahmins*, what subsequently happened was that they tested the truth of his promise and he came back and cursed them and refused to give them land and when they , terrified, sought forgiveness, he awarded them redemption from the curse. This is all that the text '*Sahyadrikhandam*' says about *Parashurama*'s gifting. Therefore it is concluded that he had never done this particular gifting. If at all it happened, it must have come about midway through. In that case, when did it actually happen? At his first leaving or when he came back to curse? Why was it not specifically mentioned in the text? Further he was not particularly in need of doing a new gifting at that point of time.

Besides, if he had already given the land to them, what was the need for him to refuse the land on his second arrival? If he refused after the gifting was over, then he was being preposterous; unreliable, contrary to his often-made statement that his words would come true without fail; and would also be incurring the sin of taking back what had been given as free gift. Moreover after the gifting was over, he could have rightfully protested and reversed his decision when he was asked by the sages to vacate the place immediately. Even at that time he did not choose to do so. Such a noble soul would never reverse/undo a charity he had already done.

Further, there could have been no gift- giving in his second arrival because what happened then was the cursing and his refusal to part with the land. Moreover after he was so badly treated immediately after the actual gifting, he would have been more careful with the land he subsequently created with much effort from the sea and therefore would have never considered gifting it again.

Parashurama never gave this land to anybody.

A reading of the text *Sahyadrikhandam* gives the feeling that he had grown so disdainful of the *Brahmins*, that he decided not to have any more friendship , togetherness with them or take their help. He also decided that the string that forms part of the fishing line of fisher folks is better than the sacred threads worn by *Brahmins*. From this it is obvious that he had not gifted land up till that point of time.

Not only that, he had refused land to them after cursing them that they would go through terrible sufferings from then on. When they pleaded with him with sorrow to grand them redemption from the curse, he granted them only conditional reprieve that his curse would become operative only during the *Kali yuga* and that they would, however, become praiseworthy in a different land called 'Asiprasta'. From these words itself it is clear that he had not given them any land. Besides, his words also imply that he was not happy with them being there and thought that they would not fare well in his land and would prosper if only they went to some other land.

Explanation: The refusal to grant land occurs only in the later part of *Sahyadrikhandam* which is concerned with things that happened far away and is hence undependable while dealing with matters connected with the *Malayalam* land. What is needed is reliance on the contents of *Kerala mahatmyam* , *Keralolpathi* etc.

Rebuttal: Both these documentary evidences refer to the same *Parashurama* who happens to be the owner of the lands in both cases and the one who did whatever that had happened at the two instances.

Explanation: The refusal happened over there, but here he gave the land with due formality.

Rebuttal: The person, the land, and the events referred to in *Sahyadrikhandam* and *Kerala mahatmyam* are all the same. So the two can not be considered as separate . If some one insists on keeping them as separate, since the person concerned is the same in both instances, one has to examine if the gifting that is said to have taken place here has actually happened prior to or subsequent to the curse/ refusal mentioned in the other.

If it is claimed it happened after the refusal, it is difficult to believe that. After the curse and the refusal, it is highly unlikely that he came over here to gift the land. There was also no need for that. Further, it is said that he went to do penance after the curse/refusal episode. Also the *Brahmins* who got cursed lived miserable lives till, after long years, king *Mayooravarman* and his son *Chandraangadan* arrived on the scene to restore the country and rehabilitate them. Their rise out of misery also happened according to the conditional reprieve he granted to them following the cursing. Except for the above events that happened, *Parashurama* is never reported to have carried out another gift-giving ceremony.

Explanation: The land was not given to those who were refused lands at first. Now it went to fresh arrivals of *Brahmins*.

Rebuttal: In that case, the acts such as making the sea recede, creating new land and gifting the land will appear to have been performed multiple times. The gifting for the removal of sin, making new land after the gifting and all the connected efforts in that direction will have to be considered as having happened more than once. And it would be as if the entire sequence of events right from his twenty one expeditions to destroy *Kshatriyas*, the gifting of the lands, the creation of new land, bringing in of *Brahmins*, cursing them etc have had a re-run in the same order. All this would sound nothing less than ridiculous.

Explanation: *Parashurama* had asked for separate lands for him to live on, and for gifting. The land for the first purpose extended from *Subramanyam*in the north to *Vaitarani*in the south and for the second from *Gokarnam* in the north to *Kanyakumari* in the south. As such, the two lands have got to be separate.

Rebuttal: That the land from *Kanyakumari* to *Gokarnam* was not meant for gifting is clear from the following points.1. According to mainly *Kerala mahatmyam*, this land was created for him to live on , as the land he possessed before was gifted away. 2. The version according to *Keralolpathi* etc to the effect that this land was created for gifting was debated and rejected earlier .

Also, the area from *Subramanyam*to *Gokarnam,* according to *Sahyadrikhandam,* is included in the land he first created. The same area is found to be included in the second creation also ,according to *Kerala mahatmyam* etc. The two do not agree with each other. Looked at from all angles, it appears wrong to hold that these are two separate lands and not one and the same.

If facts are as said above, it's baffling how two versions of it came to be recorded. It is not proposed to go into it here now, as it will be discussed in detail later in this narrative.

Now, Supposing it had happened before the cursing/ refusal episode, in The *Malayalam* land that formed the southern part of *Parashurama*'s land that extended from the *Sahya* mountains to the seas, one is certain that there must have been erudite and capable *Brahmins* living. There would not have been any need for him to go in search of *Brahmins* belonging to areas other than his own.

Explanation: it was because the local *Brahmins* were tainted due to gift-receiving etc.

Rebuttal: But, at that time, untainted ones were living in the midst of the tainted ones . They could have been invited.

Rebuttal : It was thought that others(tainted ones) would also join in.

Explanation: It could have been ensured that they did not come in. Further, there was no reason for the untainted ones to decline the invite. Instead of doing that ,the account of what happened thereafter as recorded was like this:

" No *Brahmins* turned up for conducting sacrifices or obsequies despite being invited. *Bhargava(Parashurama)* therefore angrily said, ' I have created a new land. But *Brahmins* refused my invite. What is the reason for that? I am going to create new *Brahmins* too'"

Would he, fuming as he was, as if he had no other option before him, have gone to the extent of converting low caste people like the fisherfolks who lived by killing living beings on a daily basis into *Brahmins*? Answer would be NO. Therefore there is no basis to conclude that what happened here happened before the episode in the north, as said in *Sahyadrikhandam.*

The above reasons go to show that the material contained in *Kerala mahatmyam* , *Sahyadrikhandam* etc do not relate to lands other than the one under discussion.

Explanation: One should not believe in statements from *Sahyadrikhandam.*

Rebuttal: Whether it is with reason or without reason that one chooses not to believe?

If it is without sufficient reason, anybody can disbelieve any document. In that case these texts will also get discarded. And all these hymns in praise of *Parashurama* and *Brahmins* will get knocked out and the truth will get established.

If it is with reason, then the reason has to be particularly made clear.

Explanation: *Sahyadrikhandam* was written by some one to bring disrepute to the *Brahmins.*

Rebuttal: But *Kerala mahatmyam, Keralolpathi* etc were written by some to laud the *Brahmins* and discredit the others.

Explanation: But what is said in works like *Kerala mahatmyam* etc about the master-servant relations between *Nambudiris* and *Sudras* is experienced to be correct even today. So, such works deserves to be trusted .

Rebuttal : A text is trust worthy only if what it states about a matter and its causative factors agrees with what is observed and what is derived through reasoning at least to a large extent if not entirely.

In *Kerala mahatmyam* and *Keralolpathi*, all matters about the southern *Malayalam* extending from *Kanyakumari* to *Kanjarote* river in the north and comprising of thirty two villages are stated in detail . But as for the Tulu land lying between *Kanjarote* river and *Gokarnam*, the description is limited to giving only the names of the other thirty two village the area comprises.

In *Sahyadrikhandam* , the boundaries are stated as from Subramanyam to *Gokarnam* and from north *Kanyakumari* which is close to *Subramanyam to Nasika thrayambakam*. But it describes in detail the thirty two villages that lie beyond *Gokarnam*. The tulu land that ends at *Gokarnam* finds place in both the above texts.

Out of these two namely *Kerala mahatmyam* etc and *Sahyadrikhandam*, which is to be relied upon?

If it is the former, 1. their accounts even about important events vary from each other and are often contradictory; 2. the main matters they deal with like the gifting of land have been already proved to be wrong; and 3. except for furnishing the names of the 32 Tulu villages, they do not give any more details.

As regards the relations between *Brahmins* and *Sudras*, what they describe do not very much tally with observed facts. For the above reasons, the texts that qualify for rejection are the ones like *Kerala mahatmyam*. On the other hand, the description given by *Sahyadrikhandam* about the land lying between *Kanjarote* river and *Gokarnam* ; the 32 villages it contained; its rivers, their names and the number of their branches; the arrival of the villagers, their practices, social hierarchies, their symbols etc and the details about the areas even beyond *Gokarnam* are very much in agreement with recorded geography and history of the places and actual observations. As such, out of these two groups of texts, the more credible and unobjectionable appears to be none other than *Sahyadrikhandam.*

Again, if *Sahyadrikhandam* also is discarded as unreliable, then we are left with no texts to rely on. Then we will have to go by our reasoning capacity, what we get to observe around, and official documents like title deeds etc. If we inspect such material we find that all the lands coming under three categories namely *Brahmaswam, Devaswam* and government-owned were in the past under the ownership of *Nair* landlords. We will discuss that in the next chapter.

If the last- mentioned evidence is also rejected, then we will have nothing to go by and will be forced to conclude that neither the kings, nor the landlords, nor the other owners of the lands have any claim to these lands.

The adoption of what is said in texts like *Kerala mahatmyam* as truth leads to disunity and mutual hatred among the people. It would cause no problem at all, if they are rejected. The quality called self respect that all people, and especially *Nairs*, should possess is not going to cause harm to anyone.

CHAPTER 4:

This *Malayalam* land did not belong to *Parashurama.*

According to the second half of *Sahyadrikhandam*, the *Malayala* land lies between Vaitarani in the north and Subramanyam in the south and *Sahya* mountains in the east and the sea in the west, in the shape of a '*Muram*' [15].

Bhargava, sitting in his place, has cursed the *Brahmins* in rage:' I will not give land to you. You will all become beggars every where'. When they pleaded with him for redemption from the curse, he granted them reprieve by stating,' You will , in *Kali yuga*, flourish in the place called Asiprasta'. So saying he disposed them off and the place where they subsequently arrived from there is this *Malayala* land.

This is a proof that this was not *Parashurama*'s land.

Explanation: The *Malayali Brahmins* can not be considered as the ones who went through all that. The cursed one would have gone to *Asiprastham* itself. It must be somewhere else.

Rebuttal: These *Brahmins* first occupied the northern side of *Mangalapuram* river. Then in search of livelihood and home they have travelled south. In that case they could have only come to this land.

Besides, *Sahyadrikhandam* says:' These ones carrying the curse of *Parashurama* and who are fond of *Sudra*-given food, crossed over the *Shooktamati*river(*Mangalapuram*) and reached the southern areas where, in South *Kanyakumari* exists *Agastyakooda*[16] and where live *Nayakas* the famed chieftains or land-barons of the area, and there they earned their bread by doing different jobs.

The book *Malayadri mahatmyam* describes the boundaries of this land as follows:

'*Kanjarote* river in the north, *Kanyakumari* in the south, *Malaya* mountains in the east and The sea in the west'.

The same work tells of the genesis of its name and also about how it is administered.

'Because it is ruled over by the chieftains called *Nayakas* who carry invariably a sword in their hands and are adepts in its usage , it is called *Asiprastham* (*Asi* means sword and hence *Asiprastham* means land of swords or of those who carry swords).

This goes to prove that the land of *Bhargava* lay to the north of *Kanjarote* river and the *Malayalam* land lay to is south and this belonged to the *Nair* chieftains of *Malayalam* land.

But, *Kerala mahatmyam* says something else. According to it, the Gods and sages told *Parashurama* that he deserved to be the ruler and hence he was fit for coronation'. Again it goes on: ' He arrived with the villagers of the 64 villages at *Perumpuzhakal* and ruled over the land extending from *Gokarnam* to *Kanyakumari* for fifty three thousand years'.

In that case there should have been many documents that existed in *Parashurama*'s name. But the stark fact is we do not find any. Even if we consider just Travancore which forms part of the *Malayalam* land, we find that the lands come under very many different categories. A list of them goes like this:

' *Pandara vaka thottam and otti and kaanam and paatam, Perum patu, Viruthi paatam, Puthuval paatam, Kazhaka paatam, Darkhas paatam, Nenta paatam, Sanchaaya paatam, Nadu paatam, Kuthaka paatam, Onnu paati paatam, Meetedupu Paatam, Toal paatam, Payittu paatam, Vettazhivu paatam, Karikooru paatam, Pizhaya paatam, Vilaku paatam, Kandu krishi paatam, Kuthaka krishi paatam, Mel Kangaanam, sanketam, Thuram, Kudiyiruppu, Kudumba poruthi, Tiru mukha irayili, Arul irayili, Kudumba viruthi, Chavetu viruthi, Kuthu viruthi, Kodu virithi, Kuzhal viruthi, Kombu viruthi, Vallu viruthi, Vanchi viruthi, Aana virithi, Maala virithi, Shanti virithi, Kayaru viruthi, Thali viruthi, Choolu viruthi, Kazhaka viruthi, Paattu viruthi, Paalu viruthi, Paaledupu viruthi, Keelanma viruthi, Chempu pani viruthi, Kura viruthi, Odanmar viruthi, Shangu viruthi,*

Mahabharatam vaypu viruthi, Nadakaval viruthi, Vedi viruthi, Anubhoga viruthi, Parisa viruthi, Kacha viruthi, Munnila viruthi, Pazham chottu viruthi, Oozhiya viruthi, Irayili nayaru vakapadi, Manibham, Artha manibham, Tax-free sarva manibham, Brahmadayam, Devadayam, Vatta viruthi, Mutapram, Nandavanapram, Dwadasipram, Umbalam, Ubhaya umbalam, Udama umbalam, Japti, Ayal, Adima, Anubhavam, Thiruvilam, Thiru adayalam, Guru dakshina, Mandapa kura theercha, Malavaram,Vilameladi, Adiyara paatam, Raksha bhogam, Dana pramanam, Ponnitu kaaranma, Ner karanma, Kaaranma, Attiperu, Theeru vilayola, Vaayola, Kraya shasanam, Chera otti, Meelaotti, Idakaranma, Vachupatikaaranma, Anchu randu kaaranma, Kuzhi kaaranma, Melazhma, Nadukooranubhavam, Nadulkooru vayola, Kaana paatam, Otti, Uzhavu paatam, Uzhavola, uzhavotti, Pattayola, Marayam, Atotti, Nerotti, Ner paatam, Chitotti, Ravotti,Melotti, Kodalikani, Paryapadu, Panayam, Nerpanayam, Choondi panayam, Choozhi panayam, Maraya pattam, Paata otti, Maara paatam,Karanma paatam, Vachupati pattam, Kudi pati paatam, Ozhiya paatam, Varambadaka paatam, Ven paatam, Perumbata thetam, Pathivaram, Vithupathi, Vithitu kilachu pathi, Ittupathi paatam, Kayyorupathi, otti and kuzhikanam, Paatam and kuzhikanam, Kudipulli, thanathu, Kudi janmam, Ukantudama, Yapya ukantudama, namkudama, Perkooli, Arapuswamma, Kudaswamma, Perumbadapu swarupam vaka viruthi, Paaliyathe menon vaka viruthi [17]*, etc.*

Explanation: Though it is coming under different categories now, to begin with, they were *Parashurama*'s and he was in enjoyment of them. Then he gifted away all this *Kerala* land, in charity, to the people from the 64 villages. There were people like kings, ministers and other staff appointed to look after their material and spiritual needs. These lands were given to them as well as to temples and such places of worship. That is how they came to be maintained under different categories.

Rebuttal: If you traverse back in time along the path in which all these categories evolved, you can find the primary source of it all. You can do that in respect of each category. The material that one should go by are the written documents from the past. But, never for once, think that works like *Kerala mahatmyam, Keralolpathi, Jathi nirnayam* etc could substitute for such documents. Because, they were all written with different motives in mind. Such writings serve two purposes: 1. To reveal the facts and 2.To distort the facts by squeezing in untrue things in the narrative with self-serving aims. *Keralolpathi* etc belong to the second category. They contain no material relevant to these lands. As such, they do not deserve to be even glanced at when researching these facts.

But, as said before, the finances for maintenance of the kings, ministers and working staff and the *brahmaswam, and devaswam*[18] should come from these lands. To generate money, one has got to work these lands. For that, tenants would be needed . When you distribute lands for such purposes, you will prepare the necessary records too about which property was given, the person who gave and the person who received it, and the purpose of the deal etc for future reference. Those details should normally contain the name of the owner, the name of the tenant, the details required to locate the property, its boundaries, extent, the record of the successive owners/tenants and how they came to own the property, the taxes due, taxes paid etc.

But, inspection/scrutiny of such records in respect of properties held by private owners, the government, the landlords, the royalty, *devaswams*, *Dharma* muts[19],etc, yielded no evidence that they were ever owned by either *Parashurama* or the *Brahmins*. On the other hand, it is found that they all originally belonged to *Nair* chieftains.

Explanation: It is because the *Sudras*, comprising of those *Parashurama* brought from outside to serve the *Brahmins* and those born of *Brahmins* to the celestial ladies he brought in from heaven, have by foul means usurped these properties and made false records to the effect that they owned them all.

Rebuttal : This usurpation happened subsequently. In that case, the *Brahmins* should be in possession of something that shows they were the owners before that. If they say that those records were also destroyed by the usurpers, then how is it that they did not destroy the works like *Kerala mahatmyam* etc which extol the *Brahmins*. The fact that no records to that effect exist and all the records to the contrary are available both with the *Brahmins* and the *Sudras* go to prove that the charge of usurpation is baseless.

The claim is that *Parashurama* went away after entrusting the safety of the *Brahmins* to the kings and their service to the *Sudras*. Even a single reading of *Kerala mahatmyam* etc would inform you that thereafter the *brahmins* and the kings continued to occupy high positions while the *Sudras* remained lowly and subservient. Besides, there is no record to show that the *Sudras* ever caused problems to others. How is it that the *Sudras* who were slaves, with no power , money or clout happened to grab others' property? If at all that happened, how did the *Brahmins* who were so powerful let them off so easily?

Explanation: *Brahmins*, out of sympathy and affection, granted some of the *Sudras*, status, power and privileges. They in due course and in collusion with others did the grabbing.

Rebuttal: But we find in the midst of such properties vast tracts of *Brahmin*-owned lands. How did they come to be left off by these illegal occupants?

Explanation: Those *Brahmins* were so powerful that they could not be deprived of their properties.

Rebuttal: If among the *brahmins* themselves there were those who were that powerful, they could have very well driven away the intruders with the help of their friends. Why did that not happen?

Explanation: After occupying some properties they thought that it was enough.

Rebuttal: How is it that they withdrew with such a sudden change of heart ? To quote from *Saankara smriti*: ‘ When a *Brahmin* arrives, even if he is younger in age, the *kshatriya* and *Vaishya* should rise and greet him. That is their common duty. In *Kerala, Sudra* can not greet but should only stand with folded hands. Outside *Kerala, kshatriyas* and *vaishyas* are allotted *Stree karma*. To die for the sake of the *Brahmin* is the common duties of *kshatriyas* and *sudras*. Grass cutting, ploughing the land, looking after the cattle etc are the common duties of *vaishyas* and *sudras*’.

Since the above rules are already in place in *Kerala*, the *sudras* could not have done anything harmful to them.

Explanation: But they, in violation of tradition and ethics, did all this due to their greed and evil nature.

Rebuttal : The people who did that must be *brahmins*’ enemies, big cheats and monsters. In that case there wont ever be any friendship, trust or love between the two of them .

But in *Malayalam* land, traditionally, how are they treating each other? Most *sudra* households are happy about *sambandam* [20] with *Brahmins* and they practice it merrily. What is more, in certain sub groups like *Kaimals* and *Panikkars, Brahmin sambandams* are the rule. But the progeny born of *Brahmins* to *sudra* women are not entitled to a share of the father's property. If by some chance, something of that sort came the kid's way, it used to be promptly given away in charity, under the belief that *Brahmins*' wealth if allowed into the family would destroy it. When the *Namboodiri* husband arrives at the wife's house, he will be accompanied by two or three other *namboodiris* and their servants. Therefore, all *Nair* households used to have separate accommodation, kitchen, well and tanks meant for them. They could stay there as long as they wished. They were provided with everything by the wife's house to make them feel comfortable. In addition they used to get '*dakshina*'[21]for the odd rituals they were requested to perform. Usually their entry into a family heralded internal strife, loss of wealth, ignominy and evil minded offspring. In fact their arrival was like the summer fire that devastates thick forests and the lightning- strike that destroys a high-yielding coconut tree. Because of this, most of the *taravads*[22] either stand ruined or are in the process of getting ruined. But strangely the seniors in such families do not realize their follies and continue to practise the same. They give silly explanations to those who advise them against it and remain ever faithful towards the *Brahmins*. They, even big chieftains among them, unfailingly adhere to the use of phrases, subservient in meanings, while communicating with them. With their pride in being children of *Namboodiri* fathers, their love for their fathers, and their respect for them as arbiters of things, they exhibit such devotion and respect for the *Brahmins* that it remains unequalled by any other caste in the matter of their relations with another caste. That is how these two communities interact with each other. If this is how things stand today when they are subjected to the advice to the contrary by the modern progressives among them, one can well imagine how much stronger this bonding between them would have been in the past. As such, how unfair it would be to say that these people have deprived them of their wealth by foul means.

CHAPTER 5

Neither *Bhargava* nor *Brahmins* gave *Nairs* social status and privileges:

Now let us examine the position taken by *Kerala mahatmyam* etc that it was either *Parashurama* or the *Brahmins* who gave *Nairs* their status and privileges in society.

All sub groups among *Nairs* like *Kaimal, Kartha, Panikkar, Menon, Illam, Swarupam, Pallichan* etc are considered as *Sudras* and the status/privileges they enjoy as having been bestowed on them by either Parsurama or the *Brahmins*. *Kerala mahatmyam* has this dictum too: "*Nairs* are meant for service to the *Brahmins* and the *Saamantas*[23] '. If at all the masters choose to grant some of the people who serve them high positions and privileges, what would be the reason? To keep them subordinate, equal or superior to them? If it is the first, they are already so. If it is the second or third, of what use is it to them? Anyways, it does not sound like normal practice. If it was forcibly taken by the *sudras*, it is also unlikely as discussed previously.

Explanation: We hear of instances when the nobles have conferred such status/privileges to those who were subordinate to them and it is happening from the remote past.

Rebuttal:

1.Investitures and preparations for that are of different kinds. Coronation of kings is done with the due participation of priests, peoples' representatives, etc. Such participants vary in their importance and are identified by means of their designation, insignia etc.

2.In the case of places of worship, whether in the matter of routine rituals or the periodical festivals, the officials in charge of such matters, officers from government departments, and the local landlords/chieftains have their respective places in a certain order of precedence.

3. The chieftain confers awards and other recognitions on officials as well as common citizens according to the merits of their service.

Of the above three, the first two are in the nature of duties or obligations expected of the ruled by their rulers. The third is by way of a similar exercise, but it is from the rulers to the ruled. In any case those who receive such honours are considered to be a cut above ordinary folks, but are never considered to be above the persons who conferred the honours upon them.

Let us now examine some of the honours that *Nairs* enjoy and which are considered to be conferred on them by *Parashurama* or the *Brahmins*.

1. During important functions like temple festivals, the local *Nair* landlord is brought in carried on a palanquin, when others including the *Brahmins* keep waiting for his arrival, who occupy their seats only after the landlord first seats himself on his special seat and bids all the others to do so.

2. Likewise, while hoisting the temple flag, the landlord arrives on a palanquin and occupies his prime and special seat. The *Brahmins* then ask for his permission to seat themselves and only after getting it they do so.

3. During temple festivals, while the *Brahmins* keep standing among other people, the *Nair* chieftain arrives on a palanquin, enters the temple precincts first and worship the deity. Thereupon, the temple priest hands over the '*prasad*[24]' which comprises of betel leaves, areca nut etc. to him. Then he orders that others could now enter and offer worship. Then only all the rest of the people enter the precincts and offer worship.

4. During their family functions like weddings, the *Brahmins* go to the house of the *Nair* landlord and personally invite him by ceremonially offering a stack of betel leaves and request him to see to it that the function went off well with the help from the community's volunteers.

5. When hoisting the temple flag, if the *Nair* chief is by some reason not present there, the temple-in-charge calls out enquiringly and loudly, but respectfully: 'Has the protector of this place arrived?'. Only after he arrives, the hoisting ceremony is taken up.

5. After learning recitation of Vedas, *Brahmins* get tested by the local *Nair* chief, who rewards the ones who passed with things like sacks of rice, while he subjects those that failed to humiliations like being driven away right across the village river.

In all the above examples, those who receive the pride of place/ respects are the local *Nair* chieftains and those who accord them such respects are invariably the landlords subordinate to them and the *Brahmins*. In this *Malayalam* land which was being owned and protected by the *Nairs*, such formalities showing who is superior to whom used to be observed all across the different '*Deshas*[25] of the land with minor variations. The aforementioned are some of the well known instances. There are more to be told, but it is reserved for the next book.

CHAPTER 6

If what was described in the beginning was the greatness of the *Brahmins* and the lowliness of *Sudras*(supported as they are by works like *Kerala mahatmyam*), we have discussed the greatness of the *Sudras* and the lowliness of the *Brahmins* subsequently (as supported by available official documents and common experience). Of these two, if one view is found to be true the other automatically becomes untrue. Since the first view had already been proved to be baseless consequent to the trashing of the works that supported it, the second view is what is to be believed as true. When it is so, it naturally follows that all these lands in the beginning belonged to the *Nairs* and what is in possession of others today might have been received by them from the *Nairs*. Another possibility is that the *Malayala Brahmins* themselves were *Sudras* originally.

Now, let us examine if the power and privileges *Brahmins* enjoy today were originally given by *Sudras* to them, or the *Brahmins* themselves were, to begin with, *Sudras*.

Malayala Brahmin should mean *Brahmins* belonging to the *Malayalam* land. Does it mean they were ethnic *Malayalis* or who came in from outside *Malayalam*? It is learnt from ancient texts that there were initially no *Brahmins* in this land. If they are immigrants, there are so many different categories of them. They never attach the *Malayali* tag to their names. In fact many of them resent being reminded of their connections to this land. They are the ones who constantly travel back and forth between their original places and this land. But it is not the case with the ones who arrived here first. If one can conclude that they became *Malayalis* because *Parashurama* brought them and settled them down here and made such rules as to prevent their going back, it is also not possible because all those stories stand already discredited by the foregoing discussion.

Now, about this phrase, '*Malayala brahmin*' itself: *Malayalam* is said to be one among the twelve Tamil countries. Naturally, the word , *Malayalam*, belongs to *Malayalam* land. The word *Brahmin* is not a *Malayalam* word. It originated in '*Brahmavarta*[26]' and was prevalent all over '*Aaryavarta*[27]'. It derives from the Sanskrit language. Thus these two words are separated by a huge distance. The two normally should not come together. But the combination of these two words exists here for quite some time now. If you seek to find out how that happened, one would have no other explanation except what is stated below.

Before the arrival of *Brahmins* here, here were the natives of this land, who were, courageous, capable, righteous-minded, powerful and of good character, who managed and protected this land. In due course, *Brahmins*, due to reasons like poverty etc, immigrated to this land from outside. Taking offence at their odd behavior etc, they were often driven out by the natives. Yet, they returned time and again and, by adopting a pleasing demeanour, managed to settle themselves down here. Since the status of the natives was as good as or better than the *Brahmins* of *Aryavarta*itself, like we tend to glorify new literary talent by phrases like 'Modern Kalidasa' or 'Indian Shakespeare', these people had called themselves '*Malayala brahmins*' as a mark of importance and the natives themselves accepted it. This the stark fact about their history. To corroborate it further, let us go back to *Kerala mahatmyam* itself. It says:

"The *Nakas* collected themselves at *Srimoolastana* hall and addressed the *Brahmins* thus: Hey, great *Brahmins*,we are the *Nakas* of the 64 villages. This land is a gift to us from the Sea God *Varuna* . He had done so because the *Nakas* had helped *Varuna* free his body from the affliction he suffered due to some poison. If you are not returning this land to us we will release the same poison again. Hearing this and also on the intercession by sage *Narada*, *Parashurama* persuaded the *Brahmins* to part with one fourth of the land(from *Gokarnam* to *Kanyakumari*) in favour of the *Nakas* and they accordingly did".

An older version of *Keralolpathi* too carries lines to this effect.

" Long long back, did not the roaring ocean, all hands of its immobilized, withdraw itself and the king of the ocean, *Varuna*, gave it to us?"

" Is it not to the *Nakas* that *Varuna* had gifted 108 *kaatams*[28] of land initially"

"As the powerful *Nakas* angrily spoke like thunder and glared furiously at the *Brahmins*, they, getting frightened, their limbs turning limp, heads drooping, leaving their hearth and homes, not even daring to breathe, and by night, they went away taking different routes".

The book, *Kerala vilasam*, describes *Kerala* as that which shines in water.

From yet another '*Keralolpathi*': 'When the sea abandoned its forward thrust and decided to go back, it is what the king of the sea *Varuna* got'.

From some other '*Keralolpathi*': '*Bhargava* did *Tapas*(penance) before Lord *Varuna* and created 160 *kaatams* of land from the sea'.

According to *Kerala mahatmyam*:

" It is given to us (*Nakas*) by *Varuna* , long ages ago",

" So it belongs to us", said the *Nakas*

" As such, take it as given by me (*Varuna*) to the *Nakas*".

From the lines quoted from one of the *Keralolpathis* above, it becomes clear that *Nakas* were the original inhabitants of this land and prior to the creation of this land, they were the landlords of the hills that lay close to the sea. The meaning of the statement that one-fourth of the land was given to the *Nakas* will become clear from the discussion that follows.

Malayadri mahatmyam while referring to this land says:

"By reason of being protected by landlords called *Nakas* with sword in their hands"

Sahyadrikhandam refers to this land thus:

" Land being ruled by *Sudra* kings called *Nayakas*"

All these provide further proof that this land was in the possession of *Nakas* from the earliest times.

What kind of prople these *Nakas* were will be evident from the following:

Sahyadri khandam says:

' Those that are extremely pious and god-fearing, those that happen to be unique warriors and charity-minded, whose caves are resplendent with Yogis' presence, like boxes are with precious stones inside, those *Sudra* kings called *Nayakas* ever in readiness to give their all in acts of sacrifice...'

To quote from some ancient palm leaf manuscripts in '*vattezhuthu*[29]' script:-

' Hail the *Nakas*, the ones with big moustaches, broad chests, powerful physiques, sacred ash-bearing- foreheads, hands powerful enough to smash the skull of a lion in one blow, who are masters in martial arts, extremely proficient in archery and use of swords, and so acrobatic that they can spring to great heights and do somersaults in air, capable of single-handedly driving back a herd of elephants , adepts in use of fatal slingshots, and agile and trained enough to escape shots coming their ways, experts in slitting the necks of war-horses with a knife tied to their shins, who wrench out the tongues of the ones who utter untruths and so truthful themselves, god-fearing and respectful towards sagely figures and having sages, who shine like precious stones in holes, among themselves '.

'As bearers of swords, wearers of *paalathar* (A way of wearing a long cloth with the cloth kept wrapped around the waist and one end of it taken in between thighs and tightly tucked in at the back), upper garments and footwear, with upturned moustaches, warrior-like words and elegant foreheads smeared with sacred ash, with noble bearing and elegant demeanour, these *Nayakas* are worthy of the adulation of the common people'

From yet another such manuscript (in Tamil):

'We are good; we don't consume liquor
We are good; we don't eat fish or meat
We don't even glance at others' wives
We won't live, if we can't keep our word'

Yet another manuscript describes *Nakas* thus : (*The translation may be far from perfect, though not incorrect, because the songs are in Tamil* .)

'Fortitude-personified are the *Nakas*
Stupendously strong of arms are the *Nakas*
Annihilators of the evil-minded are *Nakas*
Competent and complete swordsmen are *Nakas*
Wielders of sharp swords are the *Nakas*
Of good and widespread repute are *Nakas*
Mystics and self-realized are the *Nakas*
Masterful in archery are the *Nakas*
Winning the wars with their skill are *Nakas*

Supremely sacrificing are the *Nakas*
Prostrating before saintly souls are the *Nakas*
The embodiments of righteousness are *Nakas*
Righteousness is the only way known to *Nakas*
Righteousness is their very mind for the *Nakas*
Righteousness is the soul itself for the *Nakas*
Righteousness is God Supreme for the *Nakas*
Righteousness is the only knowledge for *Nakas*
Righteousness is their very world for the *Nakas*.'

(*Translator's note: Besides, certain folk songs like Koladi pattu, Konar pattu , Perumpattipattu and some more of unknown authorship are found quoted by the swamiji. They are all in old Tamil. The meanings of many of them are not clear. All it says by way of explanation at the end is that there were many spiritually enlightened and self-realised souls living among Nakas at that time.*)

In short, the picture about *Nakas* emerging from the above works is that they were able-bodied warriors, with good expertise in martial arts , *Marma shastra*[30], acrobatics and usage of weapons like bows and arrows, lances, knifes etc. They were well informed in matters connected with elephants, horses etc and were truthful, spiritually inclined and intelligent. They never condoned acts of indiscipline, infidelity and untruthfulness. They were teetotalers, strictly moral, especially so, in their behaviour with women, and were devotees of Lord *Shiva*(*Shaivites*) and strict vegetarians. And there were among them men of high spiritual attainments like self-realised sages.

All said, we may derive the following conclusions. The *Brahmin*-word was never in use here in the earliest times. Nor did it belong to this land. It had never done anything good here. It was brought in by the immigrants to serve their own purposes and was wrongly accepted here. And therefore, this word has got to be rejected. Alternately, one can consider it as a mere surname or something like that as found in the names of foreigners and it should never be seen as signifying any high status. If one reject this word '*brahmin*', what we will be left with are suffixes like *Embran* , *Potti*, *Namboori* etc. We will discuss that in detail in the next book.

Chapter 7

What foreigners said about *Nairs* in the past.

(Translator's note: This chapter abounds in references, about thirty in number. Most of them are names of foreigners who visited this land in the past, and some are official documents of the day like government gazettes etc. It is presumed that the source documents were all in English. Since they stand translated by the Swamiji himself into Malayalam language, not only that there is no point in translating them back into English but is also fraught with the possibility of ending up with a rendering that is inferior to the original.. It would have been good if the matter could have been accessed in their originals. But it is unfortunately not as easy as that. One would not chance upon them today unless one devotes considerable time and energy towards that. But, I would think a brief summary of it will be in order here. But in so doing I will be doing what I did not want to, initially, viz. retranslating it into its original English. In this enterprise I run a huge risk. My account could be at variance with the original source material, at least in its phrasings , even if not in meanings. I have even left out the names of those authors lest I should spell them differently than their real spellings. Therefore, I have a request to make. If someone comes across the source material they may kindly prefer it to mine.)

1.When a chieftain gets killed, his followers see to it that the enemies and their countries are totally destroyed.

2.When a king ascends the throne, a certain procedure is followed. A large bowl of cooked rice will be kept before the king. The king eats a little of it and then he hands a handful of it to each of the three hundred or four hundred Nair volunteers who are already assembled before him. And they eat it. Once it is done, they are bound by an unwritten rule. That they should give up their lives, when the king dies or gets killed.

3. This is from the census report,1891, of the Madras state. '*Nairs* are a *Dravidian* class. There are denominations among them with each having a specific job/jobs assigned to it. The earliest *Nairs* , undoubtedly, would have been fighters, who would have also enjoyed ownership of lands, and fought wars when the need arose.'

4.*Nairs* might owe their origin to the *Dravidian* natives, and they must have belonged to the ones who attacked Malabar first and hence would have become rulers and land owners. May be because of mixing of bloods and other natural reasons, they look different from the *Nairs* of other areas of Madras state.

5.The warriors here display extreme dexterity in the use of weapons. They are landlords called *Nairs*. They start their martial training at the age of seven in '*kalaris*[31]'. There, the masters apply oil on their bodies , massage firmly and make their joints and muscles supple and strong. This enable them to perform great physical feats. They believe none can surpass them in their skills, in which they take pride.

6. ... The rulers are self-respecting landlords called *Nairs*. They hold jobs like handicrafts and farming in contempt. They excel in fighting with swords in their right hands and shields in the left.

7.You wont get to see the *Nair* warriors during daytime during wars. They hide themselves away in bushes and between sand dunes. When we begin to attack, they spring forth like honey-bees from a disturbed beehive. They hold their guns well and aim targets correctly.

8. They might have been great warriors in the past. Because they are divided now due to other reasons, they are unable to stop the aggressors from abroad.

9. A *Pandya*inscription(1083 AD) says that the king annexed *Kudamalanadu* and all the *Nair* soldiers there died.

10. *Nairs* are local landlords. Fighting wars is their only job. They always carry weapons like swords, arrows, bows, spear, mace etc. They are efficient and proud of their abilities. They are born of high families. Only when they are handed weapons by the king they become eligible for the title of *Nair*. From the age of seven they start their martial training. They stay away from towns and live in their separate but protected estates. When they travel, they would shout loudly for others like farmhands to stay away from their paths. They are obeyed also. Failure to obey would entail instant death for them at the hands of the *Nair*. If a lowly person happens to touch one of their women, she is killed by her relatives at once. The offender and all his kin also get killed. This is to avoid mixing of bloods, they claim. These *Nair* women are finicky about their personal hygiene and cleanliness. They wear dresses adequately.

11.*Nairs* are warriors. One can tell them from the others by the fact that they always carry weapons with them. They are very proud of themselves. They have powers to kill certain people. No complaint stands against such killing. They are dedicated to their masters, but are often unkind with their subordinates.

12. It is believed that *Nairs* are related to *Naikkers of Vijayanagar* .Some kings of the minor kingdoms of Madura used to have the title *'Kartha'* , a denomination among *Nairs.* This title was used by the descendants of the *Naiker* kings of *Tanjore and Madurai,* according to the 1901 census.

13. *Nair* women are the prettiest among all the women of India. They keep their body and hair clean and apply perfumes to them. They never wear unclean cloths.

14. From earliest times to the end of the 18thcy, *Nairs* helped keep the land free of the misrule of the main king by administering smaller units like *'thara'* and *'Naadu'* themselves. That is how big commercial centres like Calicut emerged. *Nairs* generally held positions of overseers and jamindars.

15. An entry in the Telichery godown diary(year 1746) states: As the *Nairs* happen to be the leaders of the people of Kozhikode, their position is similar to the parliament members of England. They do not obey all the orders of the king. They punish the ministers who do unfair things.

16. The system followed in Malabar was similar to the feudal system that existed in France.

17. They specially engage themselves in body building exercises during the cool month of *Karkidakam.* Some of the physical feats they perform are mind-boggling.

18. Without bathing and changing, *Nairs* do not eat food. After bathing, they visit the temple at least once every day. Most days, they even take bath twice.

Some of the remnants of the games and physical exercises that were prevalent in ancient Greece and Rome are found among *Nairs.*

CHAPTER 8

About the *Sudra*-word

All the confusion hereabouts is caused by the two words-*Malayala Brahmin* and *Malayala Sudra*. That the first one needed to be rejected was shown in chapter 6. Let us now deal with the word '*Sudra*'. *Malayali Brahmins* call *Nairs* as *sudras*, not only in speech but in their writings too. These people too silently accept it possibly due to ignorance or lack of knowledge of ancient texts. The usage has become so common that *Nairs* themselves use it in conversation and even in official documents. At this point, a critique of the accounts of the arrival of *Nairs* according to *Kerala mahatmyam* and *Keralolpathis* would not be out of place. Let us examine if the word *Sudra* was in use here from the beginning or it came in midway through. According to *Kerala mahatmyam*, three sets of women were brought in by *Parashurama* to be coupled with the *Brahmins*. The first set consisted of the three ladies *Devendra*, the celestial king , gifted, viz.*Subhaga*(daughter of *Jayantan*), *Shubha* (daughter of *Gandharva*), and another woman of demonic birth. Each of the above three was accompanied by six damsels who formed the second group. The third group consisted of women- domestic- helps brought in from elsewhere. But the *sudra*-word is never found used as associated with any of them anywhere in those books. Even while settling them down here, this *sudra* word is not used. It only means that even while on their way this word did not attach itself to them.

Kerala mahatmyam just says that these domestic helps , both male and female, were brought from outside. But *Keralolpathi* says that *Bhargava* brought in people of *Vellala* community from *Karakkadu* and they later became the *Nairs* of Kiriyat denomination. If it is so, since all the lands from *Karakkadu* down to *Kerala* are Tamil lands, this word '*sudra*' which is alien to Tamil would not have been in use either there or here.

What needs to be addressed now is if this word came to be used immediately after their arrival here or it came in recently. In none of the writings and official documents this word appears. The army is called '*Nair* army' and not '*Sudra* army'. *Pada Nair* kulangara, *Nair kulam,* and *Iraai Nair kulam*(Ernakulam or Cochin) etc which are names of places contain only the *Nair*-word and not the *sudra*-word. But only during the last fifty years or so, this word is found used, especially in the registered sale deeds and related documents of the Travancore area. Doubtlessly, *sudra* word is of recent origin. It does not belong to this land either. From the denomination '*kiriyam*' downwards it is found used and they too did not object to it. That does not mean that the word has connections with them.

Like the words *Namboori, Bhattar, Potti* etc are used in respect of *Brahmins*, only words like *Nair, Pilla, Kartha, Kaimal, Menon*etc are used in respect of *Nairs.* None uses the *sudra* word to address them. It looks like some stupid fellow used it first in documents to be registered and the other stupid fellows who came in after continued with it.

Let us examine the language to which this word belongs. *Manusmriti*mentions *Brahmin, Kshatriya, Vaishya* and *Sudra* as the four castes.

'Hey, *Sudra*, what a pity...' (*Chandogya Upanishad*)

' The *Sudra* class was created' (*Brihadaaranyaka Upanishad*)

Certain synonyms of it are available in '*Amarakosha*'.

All these references to the *sudra*-word are found only in Sanskrit works. In the grammar books of the twelve languages(including *Malayalam*) that go by the common name 'Tamil', this word is mentioned as an alien word, that too in its mutilated form. It proves it is not Tamil, but is proof enough that it is a Sanskrit word .

Where exactly is this word being used? It is used to refer to the fourth caste in the four caste system . To enumerate the characteristics of this caste, a detailed description of the four caste system is very important and called for. And it is what is going to be attempted in the next chapter.

CHAPTER 9

The Quartet of Castes or Chaatur varnyam

Chaturvarnyam simply means *chatur varna*m meaning 'four castes'. It could be divided into two types. One, based on the aptitude and the nature of activity of the person concerned and the other based on the actual means of livelihood the person happened to choose. But the fact remains that a real classification like this can not per se be faulted as being improper or as not leading to all round welfare or as something that can be escaped without at least virtually experiencing it.

What obtains today in society is not based on the 'aptitude and action' (*guna-karma*) principle. It belongs to the second category which is the very negation of the first. It is based only on caste names viz. *Brahmin, kshatriya, vaishya* and *sudra,* and hence detrimental in effect and against the spirit of what was originally intended by its progenitors. What is being practiced today amounts to prostituting the original concept. If the first type of categorization is 'nectar', the second one is poison. If the first is like mother's milk, the second is like blood coming out of chopped-off breasts . It is the ignorance of this fact on the part of the masses and a blind belief that it is indispensable, it being law imposed by men in high positions, that makes them put up with this system.

It is based on this four- caste- division that the '*sudra*' word is being imposed on *Malayalam Nairs.* This appellation does harm them in multiple ways.For example, being subjected to misinformation, subservience, poverty, lethargy, domestic discords, loss of wealth, loss of righteousness, wrong action, atheism, irresponsible conduct etc, they become objects of ridicule before others and are being subjected to hellish experiences both in this world and the other. In order to escape this decadence, one has to first escape this offensive system which is the root cause of all the trouble. In order for it to happen, this deep-rooted misconception has to disappear. If that is to become a reality, we should become aware of the blemishless four-caste-division propounded by the sages through the *Smritis*and the deleterious system now in place in its place and the qualities of its authors. This fact has to be swallowed first if the other medicines are to take effect. Therefore, the facts about both the systems are being discussed below in the light of observed facts, its theory, and rationale.

First we will discuss the system based on 'aptitude and action' (*guna-karma*). For that we have got to think about the following in their order, viz. Common name, specific name, its author, the time of its introduction, its use, its basis, its eligibility, its practice, its comparative study and its extent.

1.General name

The text *Amarakosha*m says: ' Progeny, *gothra(sect), birth, caste, abhijanam, anvayam (race), vamsam(lineage), anva vayam, and santaanam(children)* are nine terms which are widely used among all the four castes. '*Varna*' is the word which is common for the four castes'.

In the expression '*varna* stutou', *varna* means 'praising', 'adulation'".

'*Kapila aruna peeta krishna varnai nirupyanta ithi*' means ' that which is being praised with the *Varnas* (colours) , *Kapila*(the colour of '*Gorochana*', a fragrant extract derived from cow's bile), *Aruna*(lightly reddish), *Peetha* (yellow) and *Krishna* (dark)'.

Vishnu puranam says : ' The *varnas, kapila, aruna, peetha, and krishna* separately represent *Brahmin, kshatriya, vaishya* and *sudra* in that order.

2.Specific name

'*Brahma Kshatriya Vaishya Sudra*'---(Smriti)

Brihadaaranyaka Upanishad says *Brahmin* was created first, to be followed by the three other classes (*kshatriya, vaishya, sudra*) subsequently.

It means the specific names it includes are *Brahmin, kshatriya, vaishya* and *sudra.*

3.Place of origin.

The *Manusmriti*says the system had originated in an area called *Brahmavarta,* created by the gods and inhabited by virtuous men, lying between celestial rivers *Saraswathi* and *Drishadwati.*

Therefore, it has to be concluded that the four-caste system originated in *Brahmavarta.*

4.The creator

'*Gayatri Tantra* says "It was done by the Lord"

In *Bhagavad Gita* Krishna says: " The four castes were of my creation".

5.The time of its beginning:

Since *Gayatri Tantra* says that the four-fold division of castes happened in *Treta Yuga,* it has to be considered as having born in *Treta Yuga.*

6.Its use:

*Manusmriti*says the purpose of it was the progress of mankind .

From the above paras 3 thru 5 , it is obvious that God had created this four fold system in *Brahmavarta* for the good of the mankind. Since it is for the good of mankind, it would have been equally relevant and required in the *Krita yuga* also, the *yuga* that preceded the *Treta.*

Bhaagavatam says all mankind belonged to a single class called *'Hamsas'* during the beginning of *Krita yuga.* . *Mahabharatam* declares: " Hey, *Yudhishtira,* in the beginning there was no class distinction and there was only one caste". Due to the above reasons and the statement that it was created by God in *Treta Yuga,* it is to be inferred that during *Krita yuga* this system was not in existence. Why was it not created during *Krita,* even though progress was required even then? Why at all it had to wait until *Treta yuga* for its creation? That is because *Satya*(*Krita*) was the age in which people were born with inherent righteousness in them (Bhaagavatam).. *Manusmriti*says during *Krita yuga,* righteousness(*dharma*) stood on four legs and, as such, they did not suffer from the sorrow arising out of absence of righteousness or *adharma*). That means in *Krita, dharma* was total and therefore people lived as one without any caste distinctions with pure hearts and they were virtuous and righteous. And hence they were not subjected to sufferings and they did their jobs themselves and there was no need for the four-fold division of castes.

But by *Treta yuga* they have already acquired evil tendencies (Bhaagavatam).

According to *Manu samhita,* in the yugas that followed after *Treta yuga,* people took to thieving , treachery and falsehood for acquiring wealth and education and consequently *dharma*(righteousness) suffered depletion by one-fourth every *yuga.*(That it had three legs in *Treta,* ie. *Dharma* was 75%, two legs in *Dwapara,* ie.50% and only one leg in *Kali yuga* ie. 25%). That is how this classification came into being from the age of *Treta*, and did not happen in *Krita*.

7. Its basis:

' The four classes were created by me in accordance with the people's inborn aptitude and activity. (*Bhagavad Gita*).

'Brahma created all the people who on account of their *karma*[32] acquired their castes' (*Mahabharatam*)

Due to the variation in their karmas, the caste-quartet came into being. (*Gayatri Tantra*).

Obviously the basis of the four caste system was the kind of activities people were engaged in.

8. Who got what:

According to the *Brihadaaranyaka Upanishad*, in the beginning there was only one supreme effulgence called '*Agni Purush*'. Then the creation of the universe started with the creation of the gods. *Agni purush* first created *Kshatriya* gods such as *Indra, Varuna, Yama, Easana, Mrutyu* etc. Then He created *Vaishya* gods like *Vasus, Rudras, Adityas, Viswadevas, Marutas* etc. Realising the need for servant gods, he created *Sudra* gods too. *Pooshavu* is such a god. The earth itself happens to be *Pooshavu*.

Further, according to *Mahabharat* itself, the *Brahmins* who, contrary to their own *dharma*, were given to worldly pleasures, and were adventure-minded and easily angered and thus possessing the '*Rajo guna*' became *Kshatriyas*. Those *Brahmins* who chose to rear cattle and plough the land, possessed of a mixture of Rajo and *Tamo gunas*, became *Vaishyas*. And the ones among *Brahmins* who committed murder and were untruthful, unclean in habits and ready to stoop to any level to earn a living became *Sudras*.

From these, it becomes clear that it was the innate quality of the person that decided his caste.

9.What is in practice:

Certain quotes from sacred texts again:

"There is no difference based on class/caste. The whole world forms part of Brahman. *Brahman* created everyone in the beginning. They acquired their castes due to their individual karmas. (*Mahabharat*)

'Sudras are also Brahmins. Brahmins are also Sudras. Know that Vaishyas and sudras are also similarly so' (*Manusmriti*)

The following quotes are from the *Anushasan Parva of Mahabharat*, where this fact is described in detail.

'O Mother Goddess, On the strength of the aforementioned karmas and righteous behavior, *Sudra* becomes *Brahmin* and *vaishya* becomes *kshatriya*'.

'O Goddess, Even a *Sudra* born of a lowly caste will, through the right practices , get the right knowledge and purity and become a *Brahmin*'.

'Even if he is a *brahmin*, if he is given to evil ways and eats from all, he will become a *Sudra*'.

'O Goddess, That even a *Sudra* who through right practices has become virtuous and has conquered his senses deserves to be respected as a *brahmin* is the Divine Rule'.

'Whichever *sudra* is pure at heart and in action, he is nobler than a *brahmin*'.

'One's birth, caste, scriptural knowledge, and religious practices can not be grounds for claiming the status of a *Brahmin*. The only basis for that is one's own practices'.

'All the people in this world can, through right practices, become *Brahmins*. Even a *sudra* with good practices becomes a *brahmin*'.

‘ *Brahman* is the same everywhere and for all. Whoever carries within him the Brahman that is the purest and that transcends the three *gunas* happens to be a *brahmin*’.

‘The significant ways by which a *sudra* can become a *Brahmin* and how a *Brahmin* through corruption of his qualities becomes a *sudra* were explained by me to you’

Again, some more quotes from the *Mahabharat*:

‘Whoever possesses such qualities as truthfulness, charity, patience, righteousness, compassion, calmness, and austerities is a *Brahmin*’.

‘ Whoever has conquered his sense organs, whoever adopts right practices , study the scriptures, and keeps feelings of attachment and anger under control, such a person is a *brahmin*’.

‘Whoever considers others as equals, loves a righteous life and is aware of what is right and wrong, such a person is considered a *Brahmin* by even Gods’.

Again in the *Aaranya Parva* of the *Mahabharat*, in the course of the interaction between *Yaksha and Yudhishtira*, the same subject finds mention.

Yaksha asks of *Yudhishtira*: ‘ O King, tell me unambiguously. On what factors does *brahmin*hood depends? Whether it is based on the caste one is born in, or his activities, or on his scriptural knowledge?

Yudhishtira replies thus:

‘ Neither one’s caste nor one’s erudition in the Vedas can be the basis for *brahmin*hood. The only basis is the righteousness of one’s life’.

From the above, one thing is clear. Whether one is born of a caste meant for a particular job or is engaged in a job of his own choice, he can belong to another caste by choosing the relevant field of action. It means since the high caste man can transform himself to low caste and vice versa, the factors that decide one's caste are his innate aptitude and activities.

10.Comparative study:

From the face, hands , thighs and feet...(*Manusmriti*)

Purusha sukta says ' *brahmin, kshatriya* and *vaishya* are respectively the face, arms, thighs (of *Brahman*) and *sudra* is born from his feet'.

This means the relative importance between the four castes is similar to that between the four limbs mentioned.

According to *Manusmriti*, a child born of a father and mother, lower in caste than the father , belongs to the mother's caste.

'Also, a *sudra* , even if he performs the duties of a *Brahmin*, does not become a *Brahmin*, simply because he is not authorized to do so. A *Brahmin* choosing the vocation of a *Sudra* does not become a *Sudra*, because he belongs to a high caste. It is decided by the *Brahman* this way'.

In the light of these arguments, *Brahmins* believe that there is an immutability about the four castes and hence irrespective of the aptitude and the nature of work chosen, the caste remains the same as the one you are born into.. Now, let us examine how valid the above view is. It calls for a little introduction.

Sanskrit words are of four different kinds, *Naamam*(noun), *Akhyatam* (verb), *Upasargam*, and *Nipatam*(conjunction or a word that joins other words, phrases etc). *Namam* itself is further divided into four, viz. *Jati sabdam, Guna sabdam, Kriya sabdam, and Samjna sabdam*. Apart from these, there are three other classifications such as *Shaktam, Lakshakam, Vyanjakam*, of which *Shaktam* alone is relevant to our discussion.

Shaktam or Shakti is defined as follows. 'It is the meaning that comes to the mind when one hears the sound'. It is that quality of the sound that produces a sense of its meaning. Some others define it thus: ' It is the relation with the object or objects that forms the reason for remembering the meaning upon hearing a sound'. This *Shaktham* or *Shakti* is supposed to possess two qualities about it or have two aspects to it viz. *Roodi (Samudaaya shakti)* and *Yogam(Avayava shakti).* These two *Shaktis,* independently and in combination with one another, go to form four different kinds of *Shaktam* or *Shakti* viz. *roodam, Yogaroodam, Yougikam, and Yougika roodam.* The following are the four different ways of figuring them out.

1.*Roodam*: It is that quality which gives a sense of a word's meaning thru its roodam *Shakti* irrespective of its *Yogam shakti* . Its example is the word 'Jal' which means water. It is understood as such immediately on hearing it without the need for examining its form too closely.

2.*Yogaaroodam*: It is the word which carries its roodam meaning also in its yoga meaning. Take the word '*Pankaj'* meaning lotus. Its form when dissected means 'something born in muck'. It is interpreted as meaning lotus.

3.*Yougikam*: It is the word which has only its *Yogam* meaning. Take the word *'Paachak'* which means chef or cook. Its form does not matter much. It is understood as meaning cook.

4.*Yougika roodam:* The word in which its rooda meaning and *Yogam* meaning are independent of each other. An example of it is the word *'Ulfith'*. Which means 'that which breaks out and goes up' and hence it stands for flora and fauna.

Today's *Brahmins* claim as follows. The caste names such as *Brahmin* etc are *'roodam'* in their nature. There is no point in looking for their '*Yogam*' meaning. Just like the names ,elephant, horse etc stand for different species of animals, the terms *Brahmins*, *kshatriyas* etc also stand for different and distinct kinds of human beings. Only gods and sages know the real meanings of these caste names. And therefore lower castes can never transform themselves into higher castes and vice versa. Only the successive generations of a person belong to his caste.

That this contention is fallacious is proved below. According to sage *Patanjali*'s work on Sanskrit grammer, *Maaheswara sutra and Shaakatayana's* work on grammer, words are not born just like that; that is, they are not born in a random way. Even today, Sanskrit lexicographers like *Bhanudeekshitar* do not omit even a word without interpreting their '*Yogam*' meaning. Therefore, no word can exist without its '*Yogam*' meaning. Due to lapse of time , the reason for the evolution of certain words would have become lost or unclear and hence they would have been classified as '*rood*'. But, *rood* does not indicate unknown reasons or absence of reasons. It indicates only unavailable reasons.

Their external form should have a definite bearing on what they mean. It may be that the relation between the form and the meaning is not quite obvious at the first glance. But it just can't mean there is no such relation.

Now, it will be shown that these sounds such as *Brahmins* etc do not belong to the '*rood*' category.

According to *Manusmriti*, the word *Brahmin* signifies that the person is born from *Brahman*'s face, he is the first-born and the one who carries the brahma or veda.

Similarly the word *Kshatriya* combines *Kshatam* meaning harm or injury and *Thranan* meaning protection. As such the word means one who protects from harm and injury (*Panini sootra*). Its synonym is Raja or King. It, according to *Mahabharata*' means the one who protects and provides harmony. It is hence very clear that this word does not belong to the '*roodam*' category.

Vaishya is derived from the root '*Visha*' and *visha* has the meaning also of one who has entered upon different jobs. Some of its synonyms carry meanings like rich man and trader. And hence this word reveals its meaning very clearly as not belonging to '*rood*'..

Sudra comes from root '*Shucha*' which means one who suffers or is sorrowful (*Vedanta* sutra of *Vyasa* or *Brahmasutra*). Sankaracharya's *Sutra bhashya* and other dictionaries too support this. May be because the *sudra* is supposed to do hard and menial sort of jobs, it is likely that he is sorrowful and suffering. Thus we find this word also very explicit in its meaning.

All this indicate that the sounds standing for the four castes are not without their '*Yogam*' meaning. Hence they can not be termed as '*rood*' words.

11.Lands coming under the four-caste-system and its laws:

The land lying between *Saraswati* and Drishadwati and that is created by gods is '*Brahmavarta*' (*Manusmriti*). *Kurukshetra, Matsya desh, Panchala desh* and North *Mathura* where god-realised sages live are not as revered as *Brahmavarta* (*Manusmriti*). The Madhya desh land lies bounded by Himalayas, Vindhya mountains, and is east of the land where the mythical *Saraswati* river disappeared and to the west of *Prayag* (*Manusmriti*). Aryavarta is that land that lies between the seas in the west and the east through the middle of the above mountains and it is the abode of great souls (*Manusmriti*).

The places where deers of the *Krishna sara* variety freely roam about are the fittest ones for conducting sacrifices or *yajnas*. Other places are considered impure (*Mlecha*) for the purpose.

Brahmavarta is the place of origin of the four-caste system. The sages , when the area began to fill with people, migrated to nearby unpopulated areas to do their penances. So this place lying to the south-east of *Brahmavarta* came to be known as *brahmarshi desa* or land of the sages. Its northern point is *Kurukshetra* (which included Hastinapura to the south-east of *Brahmavarta*). Its middle areas included Panchala *desa* and Madura. To its south was *Matsya desa. Viratam* lying to the west of Darlapur and 40 miles north of Jaipur was the main centre of this region. When it too became populated the sages travelled to places like *Kosalam*. Since it came into being in the middle ages and it lies central to the sea on the east and west, these areas which included *Brahmarshi desh and Kosalam*, came to be christened '*Madhya desh*'(or central region). Its boundaries are Kurkshetra in the west, Prayag in the east, Vindya ranges in the south, and the Himalayas in the north. Here too, it was the sages who first occupied the northern banks of river Ganges and subsequently only they happened to occupy its southern banks in search of peaceful surroundings. This is obvious from the descriptions in *Valmiki Ramayana* etc, that Ayodhya city was on the northern side and the hermitages of sages like *Viswamitra* were on the southern side of the river. This central region became highly populated in time. Here the four caste system was prevalent. Those who were part of the system were called *Aryas* and those who stayed away were called *Mlechas. Arya*means knowledgeable person. *Mlecha* means one who is not capable of good conversation. Since *Aryans* lived here, it was called Aryavarta. The other places were called by them as *Mlecha* lands.

The system of the four castes and its attendant laws belong exclusively to the lands lying between the two seas, the Vindhyas and the Himalayas.

From the above, it has become clear that God who controls the entire universe, seated himself in *Treta yuga* at *Brahmavarta* and established the four-caste-system , based on aptitude cum activity, as law that applies not only to *Brahmavarta* but also to *Aryavarta*, in such a way that the relative order of the parts of a body viz. face, hands, thighs and feet goes by the general name of '*Varna*' and specific names of *Brahmin, kshatriya* , *vaishya* and *sudra.*

Since the *Malayalam* land does not come within the above mentioned territories, it also follows that such laws are not applicable here. While those that belonged to the above regions considered those from elsewhere as 'mlechas'or plebians, they have referred to *Malayala Nakas* using terms more respectable than words like *mlechas* initially. It only shows that they accorded *Nakas* a relatively high status in early times. It only proves that nobody , even under traditional powers , though rejected on the basis of experience and documents, can impose this *Sudra*-word upon the *Nairs.*

Besides, since, differences in *varna*s are part and parcel of nature, no community of people can claim superiority over another, in support of which the following matter is also adduced.

Taithariya Brahmanam says: '*Brahmin* is born of *Sama* veda, *Kshatriya* of *Yajur* veda and Vaishya of *Rig* veda. In Shaiva system, it is from Lord *Shiva*'s limbs, in Vaishnava system it is from Lord *Vishnu*'s, and in the *Saktheya* system it is from *Shakti*'s. Factoring in all this, one has to conclude that the *varna* differences were meant to make the world more acceptable for living. In accordance with that principle, changes take place all over at all times. The evil effects of the domination by the priestly class apart, this truth was known in this land itself from the distant past. For example , take a look at the identifiable signs of a *Brahmin* as provided by *Gautama samhita.* The attributes prescribed are same as what was told in the verses of Mahabharata quoted earlier.

In fact , as mentioned in *Brihadaaranyaka Upanishad*, the four castes are found to exist among even Gods. Animals, reptiles and even musical notes are found to be traditionally classified this way.

To put things in perspective, the four-fold classification is based only on one's inborn aptitude cum action chosen . As such only people with the characteristics pertaining to a particular *varna* (caste) become eligible for inclusion in that *varna.* Without those characteristics, one can not belong to a *varna* even if one is born of parents of the same *varna.* If a person born in a particular caste having its own peculiar traits do not possess those traits, but possess traits of another caste, then he belongs to the latter caste only, irrespective of considerations of which is higher or which is lower. This has also been found practiced in the past. If one goes for a norm other than this one (aptitude cum work) for such classification, it will not only be baseless, but will bring about intermixing among classes and it will result in a situation like what it was before this 4-castes came into being.

What prevails today is just that. It constitutes the earlier-mentioned second category that is adopted purely as a means of livelihood. We will discuss its features in the next chapter.

CHAPTER 10

The misuse of the four caste system and *Brahmin*ism

The existing practice is like this. If a *Brahmin* marries a *Sudra* woman and a girl child is born of that union, and that girl too marries a *Brahmin*, and this process continues for seven generations, the child belonging to the seventh generation will become a *Brahmin*. But a male child born of such union can only be *Sudra*. For *Kshatriya-Sudra* and *Vaishya-Sudra* unions, this transformation from one caste to another happens in the fifth and third generations respectively.

As such, the children born to *Brahmin* parents would only be *Brahmins*. For assessment of the development of communities, one needs to find out the caste and we have to find some way of figuring it out. Since it is found that a *sudra* adopting a *brahmin*'s work does not become a *Brahmin* and vice versa, the vocation of a person can not be considered as a guide to it. The *guna-karma*(aptitude cum action) principle apart, the only way to find it out is by means of the '*rood*' principle. But it has already been proved that it was baseless. If we think of adopting the kapila-crimson-yellow-black colour scheme for it, it will not be of any use because colours are misleading and confusing.

What we show below are some of the age-old rules that insist that it is only the aptitude cum action principle, and not birth or tradition, that should form the basis for determining the caste.

1.From *Anushasan parva* of *Mahabharatam*:

Sage *Viswamitra* , born as *Kshatriya*, later became a *Brahmin* and indeed turned out to be a progenitor of the *brahmin* caste.

2.From *Vishnupuranam*:

Pradirathan is *Kshatriya*. His son *Kanua*'s son is *Metadidhi*. It is from him that the entire *Kanuaayana Brahmins* originated.

Mahaveerya is a *Kshatriya*. His son has three sons. These three became *Brahmins* at a later date.

3.From *Bharatam Harivamsam*, chapter 32:

Mitrayu, the *Kshatriya*, became '*brahmarshi*'(a sage of the highest order). His son Maitraayanan had a son by name Soman. He established the clan of *Maitreya Brahmins*.

It can not be said that only *kshatriyas* alone became *Brahmins*. Even people born of low castes have become *Brahmins*. To quote from *Sahyadrikhandam* :

'In that land without *Brahmins*, *Bhargava* espied fishermen. He took the string from their fishing lines and made them wear it as the sacred thread'.

Numerous instances of not only conversions from one caste to another on the basis of *karma* or vocation, but also instances of one race giving birth to all the four castes can be cited from *Bharatam* , *Vishnu puranam* etc

4.From *Vishnupuranam*, Amsa 4, chap 1:

Vaivasvata Manu is *Brahmin*. From his son '*Karusha*' came *Kaarusha kshatriyas*. Another son of his was *Nedishta*. *Nedishta*'s son became *Vaishya*.

Yet another son of his by name '*Prushodran*' became a *Sudra* because he killed the cow of his master.

5.From *Vishnu puranam*, Amsa 4, chap 8:

Sunahotra has three sons: *Kaasan, Lesan, Grilsamadan. Grilsamadan's son is Shounakan. Shounakan*'s children belonged to the four castes.

In '*Harimamsam*', the name Lesan becomes *Shalan*, and *Shounakan* becomes *Shunakan*. It says: *Grilsaman's son is Shunaka. Shunaka*'s progeny belonged to the four castes.

Bhaargan's son is Bhaargabhumi, from whom came children belonging to the four castes.

6.From *Bharatam Harivamsam*, 32nd chapter:

The progeny of sage '*Angiras*' belonging to the *Bhrigu* clan became *Brahmins, kshatriyas, vaishyas* and *sudras*.

7.From the same text, 11th chapter:

'Two *Vaishyas* who were the sons of *Naabhagarishta* became *Brahmins*'.

Naagaabhishta was the grandson of *Vaivaswata Manu.* A man of such noble lineage as him became a *vaishya* on account of his less- than- noble character, while his sons who were by birth *vaishyas* became *Brahmins* by taking up the right professions.

From this it is obvious that even members of a clan who became low caste people due to their evil habits can convert themselves back into higher castes through performance of good deeds. What all this points to is the fact that it is only action, not birth, that decides one's caste. In support of this, here are some quotes from the Vedas.

8.From *Koushitaki Brahmanam*:

Once, a person named *Kavasha* was sent out of the sacrificial grounds, whose main priests were sages *Grilsamada, Visvamitra, Vama deva, Athri, Bharadvaja, and Vasishta*, on account of his being born to a servant maid. He prays to Goddess *Saraswati* who appears before him and takes him to where the *Yajna* (sacrifice) is being held. Upon seeing him in the company of the goddess, they receive him warmly , accord him high honours and makes him the main priest of the event.

This story finds place in *Aitareya Brahmanam* too.

9.*Koushitaki Brahmanam*, Panchika 2, chapter 3:

Some of the great sages began a sacrifice by the *Saraswati* river. They expelled *Kavasha*n from their midst on account of his being the son of a maid servant and a *sudra* to an arid land where he would die of thirst. While suffering like that, he composed the *mantra*[33] called '*Aaponaptriyam*'.

10. The Veda tells the story of a respectable son of a *sudra*:

' O *Brahmanaspati*, May this drink of the *Soma* spirit make me as effulgent as the son of '*Ushik*' '.

That a *Sudra* is ineligible to receive spiritual initiation and acquisition of Vedic or *Brahmic* knowledge is the stand of the priestly class. With this end in view, they have gone about misinterpreting the Vedas and Vedic commentaries. In this regard, one particular story they did not find amenable to such tweaking was that of *Jaanashruti* finding place in *Chandogya Upanishad*.

Jaanashruti or *Poutrayanan* was a king. While he was asleep, three swans flew down there. He heard one of the swans saying that *Jaanashruti* was indeed great. But another swan immediately intervened and said, 'How could this illiterate person become great? Only *Raikva* is great'. *Jaanashruti* caught with the desire to acquire Supreme knowledge at any cost, approaches sage *Raikva* with cows and gold as offerings. But *Raikva* rebuffs him by calling him *Sudra* , refuses to teach and turns him out saying 'Hey *Sudra*, keep your cows to yourself'. The snubbed *Jaanshruti* goes back, but returns again , this time with more offerings. It included his lovely, unwed daughter, one thousand cows and some chariots. But this time *Raikva* has no hesitation to accepting all that. He then proceeds to impart to him the knowledge that he was after.

11.*Sama* veda-*Chandogya Upanishad*-Samvarga vidya-the story of *Jaanashruti*:

(Translator's note: This portion contains only the source text in Sanskrit , narrating the above story of Jaanashruti)

12. Brahma sutra and Sri *Sankara*'s interpretation:

What is shown below are the writings and their interpretations made with the intent of giving the *sudra*-word that occurs in the Sanskrit source text a wrong meaning. *What immediately follows is the interpretation of Jagadguru Sri Sankara.*

"Sutra[34] 34 :

Just because man is entitled to knowledge, there is a view that *sudra* is also entitled to knowledge in the same way as the gods are entitled to it. This is just to dispel this notion.

Sudra has the right to knowledge. There appears to be no denial of access to knowledge to a *sudra* in the same way he is denied sacrificial rights. It is true that he lacks '*Agnituam*'[35]. It only bars him from performing sacrifices. But it does not deny him access to the knowledge of it. Nor does it imply that he is incapable of learning such stuff. When *Jaanashruti* approaches *Raikva* for knowledge, the *Sudra*-word he utters while insulting him by saying, 'Hey *Sudra*, keep your cows to yourself' becomes a subject of much debate. Though *Vidura* etc were born *sudras* they were considered eligible for knowledge acquisition. On the basis of the above-stated reasons, if *sudra* becomes eligible for knowledge, then I have to say this. Just because *Sudras* have no right whatsoever over Vedas, they can not seek to acquire knowledge of it. Those who studied Vedas alone can have the right for interpreting its meanings. *Sudra* can not learn Vedas because they do not go through the rites of passage like *Upa<u>n</u>ayana*[36], which is only the prerogative of *Brahmins*, *kshatriyas* and *vaishyas*. When he lacks eligibility, the craving for knowledge alone can not constitute the basis of his right to knowledge. Since he is denied knowledge, he stands denied of the eligibility for it too. By whichever rule he becomes ineligible for sacrifice, by the same rule he stands ineligible for knowledge.

Just because *sudra*-word occurs in the story, one can not think *sudra* is entitled to knowledge. Not only that it relates only to the *sudra* who appears in the narrative. Because the words of the swan (quoted above) makes him sorrowful. Here when he is addressed as *sudra* by *Raikva, Raikva* only means the knowledge-seeker was sorrowful.(because the *sudra*-word has the meaning, 'one who is sorrowful' also). And he did not use it as meaning '*sudra*-by-birth'.

Sutra 35:

According to this sutra too, *Jaanashruti* is not a born-*sudra*. Because towards the second part of the *Jaanashruti* story, due to the association with the name of *Chaitraratha*, the *kshatriya*, *Jaanashruti* too looks like belonging to the *kshatriya* race for different reasons. Because of this reason too, the born-*sudra* does not become eligible for knowledge.

Sutra 36.

According to this rule too, *Jaanashruti* is not entitled to knowledge. It is established that for initiation into knowledge, the aspirant should have gone through *upanayana* etc. It is evident from the following example. Bharadwajis, in search of the knowledge of *Brahman*, approached '*Pipalaadan*' who is like god himself. At that time these words were heard: 'Do not give them *upanayana*'. It only shows *upanayana* is a prime requirement before imparting knowledge. Based on this saying that '*Sudra* is the fourth *varna* and a single caste', and also because he is not required to go through *upanayana* etc on account of his being without sin, it is established that he need not go through the rites of passage like *upanayana*.

Sutra 37:

This also tells that *sudra* has no right to knowledge. *Jaabala* was given *upanayana* and imparted knowledge by sage *Gautaman* only after getting him to swear on oath that he was not a *sudra*. But the fact of the matter is that none other than a *Brahmin* could make such a statement of discrimination.

Sutra 38:

This sutra too bars *Sudra* from knowledge. According to *Smritis, sudra* can neither listen to nor acquire knowledge of the Vedas. This should naturally include a bar on interpreting and practicing the Vedas. There is a rule which says: ‘ As he had listened to the Vedas, let his ears be plugged by pouring molten lead and wax into them’. Not only that, there is another rule which says that if a *sudra* utters veda his tongue should be chopped off and if he carries the veda in his person, his body should be cut open. Also the veda clearly prohibits imparting of knowledge to the *sudra* and asserts that teaching, sacrifice and gifts by way of charity are meant for *Brahmins* only. And therefore it has to be concluded that *sudra* can not claim vedic knowledge as a matter of right.”

The time when *Jaanashruti* was scoffed at (by addressing him as *Sudra*) and sent back by *Raikva* was one in which the rule that prohibited teaching of Vedas to *sudras* was very much in force. In those times, this would have certainly made *Jaanashruti* to think that *Raikva* had taken him for a *sudra*. Had he not been a *sudra*, his immediate reaction would have been one with the aim of clarifying his real caste. But he had not done that. It is enough proof that he was in fact a *sudra*.

Even otherwise, a plain reading of the story will make one believe that the *sudra*-word occurring therein could only mean ‘born-*sudra*’. The *Sudra*-word in this story causes the ancient commentators considerable consternation and confusion. That is why they embark upon their job of obfuscation and misinterpretation. These ancients themselves seem to have known very well that the reader would only take the word as meaning 'born-*sudra*'.

Or if he went away without uttering a word as he knew that *Raikva* had only meant it in its '*Yogam*' meaning(that is, as one who was sorrowful), then it is quite improbable. Because a man who was put in the downer by the mere words of the swan imputing illiteracy or ignorance on his part can not be expected to have the intelligence or literary acumen to make out what *Raikva* actually meant.

Again, if indeed he was not a *sudra* but only a *Kshatriya* as argued by the commentator, then he would have straightaway become eligible for receiving lessons. In that case what was the need for him to be turned away by *Raikva*? None, certainly. If there is some rule that excludes the sorrowful from receiving lessons, it would be most unfair. The man with the sorrow which would not go away unless taught and which constitutes the cause of the first rejection is getting imparted with the knowledge on his second visit. There is also a principle that an aspirant sorrowful about his ignorance is the fittest one to be taught.

If it was to further check his suitability, then there was no need for that for a man like *Raikva* who was in possession of supernatural powers. If such a testing was indeed unavoidable, it would only mean that *Raikva* did not have such powers and *sudra* word was not used in its '*Yogam*' meaning.

If it was meant to improve the aspirant's learning skills, it should have been done by letting him live there for quite some time followed by careful observations. It was also not done. Was it then done with the aim of extracting a higher *dakshina*[37](gifts) from the aspirant?

He did not even have the power of forethought to guess that, even if refused first , he would have to accede to his request next. It could only mean *Raikva* did not foresee anything with his inner eye, but only saw things with his mortal eyes. He had taught him when he returned with a much larger offering of gifts. He had no qualms about it. It only means that he was greedy after wealth and he was not a man of his word and was not honorable enough to want to keep the sanctity of his own word. All this points to the one and only fact that the *sudra*-word he used meant only born-*sudra* and it did not carry any figurative/allegorical meaning as assigned by later-day commentators.

Here the master had no qualms about imparting knowledge to a *Sudra* when he was presented with gifts of considerable worth. From this it is obvious that being *sudra* was not such a big issue when it comes to the question of imparting the highest knowledge. To this , the explanation of the priests was that the word *sudra* should not be taken literally and it was figurative/allegorical in intent, meaning one who was unfit to be taught for some other reason. But then if indeed he was not a *sudra*, why did he not choose to clarify when he was addressed '*sudra*' by the master. What was the need for him to go back and return with more offerings. This, by itself, is proof that he was in fact a *sudra* and his getting the vedic knowledge was not such a big deal when one could afford the cost of such acquisition.

Jaabala's is another story with a similar message. It is cited as an example by the commentators themselves and it is considered as strong a case as *Jaanashruti*'s story.

Jaabala goes to sage *Gautama* for receiving *Brahmic* knowledge. But *Gautama* harbours doubts about the person's caste. But he proceeds to impart the knowledge after making *Jaabala* swear on oath that he was not a *sudra.*

That *sudra* can not be taught Vedas is an accepted fact. *Jaabala* approaches the master just for getting that knowledge. From the fact that he gets him to swear that he was not a *sudra,* it is clear that *Gautama* had doubts about his caste. Besides, *sudras* are considered untruthful in behavior. But *Gautama* just takes his word as truth. When *Gautama* could have made further enquiries and confirmed *Jaabala*'s caste, he chooses not to do so and readily agrees to teach him the ultimate knowledge sought, on the strength of a mere oath that could have been very well untrue. This also goes to prove the following things. That *Gautama* was not particularly strict about not teaching him. That he did not believe that either he or *Jaabala* would come to harm on account of such action on his part. That he did not believe that *sudras* were strictly forbidden to receive vedic education.

Explanation: But the question remains as to why he got *Jaabala* to swear.

Rebuttal : It must have been done just as an excuse to be presented before his peers of the day who were very particular about adhering to their self-made rules like '*sudras* can not learn and *sudras* should not be taught' as if those rules were so sacred that they can not be flouted. In case *Gautama* was taken to task and questioned on this score, he could always explain that he taught *Jaabala* only after ascertaining his caste by getting him to swear about it.

That the rites of passage like *upanayana* are just not enough for acquiring *Brahmic* knowledge and what in fact was required for that was the acquisition of '*Sadhana chatushtayam*' on the part of the aspirant is borne out by the following lines taken from Sri '*Vedanta bhashya sutra, chapter1, paada 1, adhikaran 1.*

(Note: *The quote is in Sanskrit and its meaning is unfortunately not furnished either in the source text or in the notes that accompany it.)*

It has already been established that the only basis for caste is the person's ' aptitude and activities' and not birth / tradition. It was also shown that castes were decided that way from the earliest times and there were inter-caste conversions on that basis. As a further support to this, we shall furnish a general description about the *Brahmin* race and about the origin of some of them who through generations pride themselves as *Brahmins*. Let the readers themselves decide how much social respectability they deserve on the basis of the separation of castes or as a caste in general.

The essence of *Sahyadrikhandam*, 2nd part, chapter 1:

Brahmins are of two kinds:

1.*Pancha dravidar, 2.Pancha gowder.*

Pancha dravidar: 1. Dravidas, 2.Thailangas, 3.karnaatar, 4.Madhya deshagans, 5. Gurjaras.

Pancha gowdas: 1.Gowdas, 2.saaraswatas, 3.Kanya kubjas, 4.Ulkalar, 5.Maidhilar.

Or

1.*Trihotras, 2.Agnivaishyas,3.Kanykubjas, 4.Kanojayar, 5. Maitranayar.*

The common rights of *Brahmins*:

1.Brahma gayatri, 2.Veda karmas, 3. Six duties starting from teaching, 4.Bhumjrutvam, 5.Bhojaneeyatvam,6. Marriage.

Their, location-based, degenerate and degrading practices:

1.In *Gurjara desa*, they drank water from receptacles made of animal hide.

2.In *dakshina desa*, they bedded lady helps.

3.In Karnataka, they did not brush their teeth.

4.In Kashmir, they worked as washermen.

5.In *Tailanga desha, govaahanam.*

6.In *Dravida desh*, they ate stale food.

7. *Gurjara* women did not cover their breasts, only widows did. *Trihotras and Kanojayas* were meat/fish eaters.

7.Among *Kanyakubjas*, sex among siblings was common
.

13.*Sahyadrikhandam*,2nd part, essence of chapter 2:

The origin of *Karaashtra Brahmins*:

The land of *Karaashtra* lies between *Vedavati* in the south and *Koyana sangamam* in the north, with an extent of ten *yojanas*. Their goddess is *Matruka devi*. They used to sacrifice *Brahmins* with perfect physical features annually to the goddess. Due to this sin, they perished.

It is said that if one happens to touch one of them, one has to purify oneself by taking bath. It is also believed that the air surrounding them gets noxious and polluted for a distance of three *yojanas*. They are barred from all religious practices and duties. Some of them carry names made up of two words.

The land of Konkana:

On *Sahyan* heights, it lies 4* 100 *yojanas* in size. They have rights over only truncated Gayatri *mantra*. They have to be eschewed in all ritual occasions.

Chapter 2 of the above work:

Govindapura gowdas are meat eaters and liquor consumers.

Coastal *Saaraswats* are fish eaters. They are of ten different kinds. It is said that, in *Vaaraaham,* they used to eat elephant meat. In *Jagannata* too they ate fish and meat. Those to the south of Narmada river used to marry their nieces.

Let us stop this narration here for the time being to be continued in the next book.

'*Kerala mahatmyam*' is supposed to be a book dealing specially with *Kerala*'s traditions and which serves as a reference guide to Keralites. Those who want to know more can refer to annexure 3[38] (which is but left unexplained).One regrets to commend that the belief system and practices prescribed and promoted by *Kerala mahatmyam* for these people were sinful and ridiculous. This book itself declares in its beginning that the original inhabitants of this land were extremely truthful and virtuous. *Sahyadrikhandam, Saankara smriti* etc also support this view. How did they fall from that high pedestal? Was it of their own making or due to machinations by outsiders? Based on our discussion so far, it has to be inferred that their hellish experiences were due to the ingress of these *Brahmins* who were expelled from their original places and who were practitioners of false religions. One can find instances in world history of civilized societies and establishments degenerating themselves by taking to evil practices due to their proximity to evil. Even the ancient epics mention about egregious people among *Brahmins* who lived before . And, so, it has to be decided whether it was such evil characters or good people who came in here. Examples to be cited in this connection are works like '*Sahyadrikhandam*' and sayings of sages *Narada* and *Vyasa*.

Arbhatiya Samhita too refers to this aspect of this land's history. Some of the extracts from the above works are furnished below.

' These dispelled *Brahmins* went without food and shelter in the beginning. Then, they headed south to the land lying between the western sea and the *Sahya* mountains, where sage *Agastya* lives, where Goddess *Kanyakumari*'s abode exists,, where the people are pious, virtuous, charitable-minded and warrior-like, where sagely men of divinity shine like precious stones in its chest, where lavish in their charitable acts live *sudra* kings called *Nakas*. These immigrants gradually ingratiated themselves in the society using fair and foul means. Some of them tricked the local landlords, some of them made money by serving them loyally, some acquired wealth through some other foul methods like engendering among the locals discord and infighting, some earned their living as cooks, some took up lowly, menial jobs. What will they not do, these curse-bearing-ones (reference is to *Parashurama*'s curse)'.

(From *Arbhatiya Samhita*, chapter 11)

What is quoted above are the words of Lord *Skanda* (*Subrahmanya*) in response to the queries of *Sathaanika.*

Sage *Narada*'s and *Vyasa*'s words: (*Translator's note: Omitted because the source text carries only the Sanskrit passage without its meaning in Malayalam)*

The consequences of rejecting the above evidence have already been explained. It is no surprise that the people described above have created such a reprehensible system as the one propounded by works like '*Kerala mahatmyam*'. Those who have gone through hardships because of such a system can only sit rueing their lack of sense and judgment now. Let us console ourselves that , at least from now on, if they perform their duties and responsibilities well, it will spell the end of their disrepute and their early grandeur will begin to shine again.

(concluded)

CHAPTER FIVE

Notes

The right to the Veda – A critique

1. *Pravachanam: Its simple meaning is Prediction. The Vedas are also called Pravachanam. May be it is due to the fact that the Vedas are believed to have been received by the sages intuitively and the matter survived through word of mouth, down numerous generations.*
2. *Puranas : Along with the Vedas and the epics, Puranas form a part of Hindu theology. There are a number of them, but eighteen of them are considered important. They deal with the mythology associated with the various deities of worship.*
3. *Brahmananda Saraswaty :An important exponent of the Advaitic(non-dual)school of Hindu thought. An author/ commentator of many works.*
4. *Kumbhipakam : One of the many Hells where the evil souls are supposed to spend time after death.*
5. *Rouravam: Another Hell like Kumbhipakam.*
6. *Saadhana chatushtayam: Saadhana means practices for the ultimate spiritual attainment of God-realization and chatur means four. The term as a whole refers to the four spiritual attainments considered as leading to the attainment of the supreme state of Enlightenment/*

Liberation. They are 1) Capacity to discriminate between the real and the illusory. 2)Loss of desire for any kind of enjoyment, either this-worldly or other-worldly. 3) Attainment of six sub-qualities under this head viz. a)Control of the five senses of perception, b)Control of the five organs of execution, c) Withdrawal of oneself from the world, d)Capacity to endure any hardship, e)Unshakable faith in the Absolute, and f)Undivided attention/ concentration on the Absolute. And finally 4)An overall disposition towards the Yogic state.

7. *Adha :it means auspicious, afterwards, a question of significance etc.*
8. *Mimamsa:One among the six systems of Hindu philosophy. The six are Saankhya, Yoga, Nyaya, Vaiseshika, Mimamsa and Vedanta. Mimamsa deals with the principles of how sacrifices are to be conducted according to Brahmanams.*
9. *Braahmanam : One of the four parts Vedas consist of , viz. Mantras, Braahmanams, Aaranyakams, andUpanishads.*
10. *Alwars and Naayanmars: The revered Vaishnavite and Shaivite saints of the Tamil country.*

The place of woman and man in the world

1.The three worlds: In Sanskrit, they are Bhoo loka, Bhuvar loka and Swar loka. Loka means world. Bhoo loka is the visible, experienced world in which we live. Bhuvar and swar are higher worlds that are not perceptible, except to the realized ones. Swar loka can be called Heaven, while Bhuvar loka is an ethereal world in between Bhoo and Bhuvar.

Compassion towards living beings

1.Pralaya : This universe and all its constituents are said to have been in an embryonic form, encapsulated as they were inside what is called 'Moola prakriti' or 'Source-Primal' or Primal nature. This state is called the state of 'Pralaya'.

Ancient *Malayalam*
Introduction

1. *Land of Malayalam : The ancient land of Kerala which lay to the south-west of India. The modern Indian state of Kerala is a fragmented version of the ancient one which was larger in extent.*
2. *Brahmins: The first among the four castes known popularly as the priestly class.*
3. *Guru: A person of considerable learning who guides others in matters spiritual and material.*
4. *Parashurama: One of the ten incarnations of Lord Vishnu. Lord Vishnu is the second in the trinity of Brahma, Vishnu and Rudra entrusted respectively with Creation, Preservation and Dissolution of this world.*
5. *Hindu: The majority religion of India.*
6. *Nair: A caste of Kerala, which traditionally occupied, in the caste hierarchy, a place just below Brahmins but above a host of other castes.*
7. *Dravidian: connected to Dravidas who are said to have been the natives of south India.*
8. *Kshatriyas: The kings or the born rulers of the land.*
9. *Yojana : A measure of land.*
10. *Vamana : Like Parashurama , Vamana is also one of the ten incarnations of Lord Vishnu.*
11. *Kali Yuga: The age of the evil or the Age of darkness. Hindu philosophy divides time into four epochs or ages, namely, Satya yuga, Treta yuga, Dwapara yuga and Kali yuga. The duration of the yugas are 4800, 3600,2400 and 1200 celestial years, respectively. (One celestial year equals 360 earthly years). !00 % righteousness exists in Satya, 75% in Treta, 50% in Dwapara, And 25% in Kali, the rest being evil.*

Chapter 1

12.Jnana, Yoga and Tapas: Jnana and yoga both signify the state of self-realisation or the state in which the individual self becomes one with the cosmic self. Two different words are employed to mean the same thing because the paths adopted are different, though the goal reached is the same. Tapas means the penances one goes through in reaching that goal.

13.Srutis : Vedas , four in number, viz. Rig, Yajur, Sama and Atharva.

14.Smrutis : Itihasas or epics like Ramayana, Mahabharata and Puranas ,generally considered as eighteen in number.

Chapter 4

15.Muram: It is a kitchen utensil, square in shape ,used for winnowing chaff out of grains etc.

16.Agastyakooda: Is a place inside deep forests , towards the south of the Sahya mountains, situated at a great height, where it is believed Sage Agastya did penance once in the past and it is accessible even today by climbing the mountains on foot only. The trek usually takes two days.

17.There are approx. about hundred and fifty classifications starting from Pandaravakathottam, listed there , under which land is held by the people. The names are in Malayalam and, to my knowledge, there are either no known English equivalents for them or are no more in use. Except for a couple or so of them which are mentioned by old timers, there is no way of finding their meanings or what they stood for. All this author knows is the word 'paatam' which occurs multiple times in the list stands for a kind of lease. Lands under 'paatam' are lease-held lands. Another word I know of is 'Oti' which stands for mortgage. Viruthi is another word that occurs several times, and, as far as I can figure it out, it stands for work or job, and so one has to presume that those lands are held for some specific purpose. For example, Chempu pani viruthi should mean works connected with copper, like making utensils etc and that land is held by someone for that specific purpose. Mahabharatam vaypu viruthi should mean land allotted to someone by way of fees for reciting Mahabharat, possibly during religious events. I am not too sure of my interpretations but I hope I am not way off the mark.

18. Devaswam, Brahmaswam : Properties of temples, Properties of Brahmins respectively

19.Dharma mut: A charitable institution.

20.Sambandam: It signifies a matrimonial union between a Nair woman and a man of her caste or a Nair. Though it is not an actual marriage in the way Brahmins conduct it, it is very much a marriage as practiced by Nairs.

21.Dakshina: It is the fees, a priest gets for performing rituals on behalf of some other person. The amount is , however, not pre-decided.

22. Tharawad: A traditional Nair household which houses a large number of the members of its joint family. Usually such a tharavad will be the wealthiest in that village with vast estates of landed property and the head of the family a VIP in that village.

Chapter 5

23. Samanta: Subordinate kings in charge of separate areas or portfolios under the chief king. ;[p0

24.Prasad ; Is something the priest hands over to the devotee as a token of the blessings of God. It normally consists of sacred ash, sandal paste, saffron, fruits, betel leaves etc.

25. Desa: Desa is perhaps the smallest administrative unit in a kingdom. The entire land is divided into divisions for the ease of administering it. They are further divided into Desas etc.

Chapter 6

26 & 27. Brahmavarta and Aryavarta: They are areas in the north of Bharat (India) of the remote past where the four caste system is said to have evolved.

28. Kaatam: A measure of land area

29.Vattezhuthu: The script belonging to the remote past, before the script of Malayalam, as available today, evolved.

30. Marma sastra: It is an old branch of indigenous medical science dealing with fractures, sprains, pains etc in the human body. Notes:

Chapter 7

31.Kalari: The dedicated ground meant for teaching martial arts.

Chapter 9

32.Karma: Its plain meaning is work, job, vocation. On a higher level it has a connotation of fate and destiny. And, as such, the good or bad experiences one goes through in life or the works /activity in which he engages himself are part of his destiny. It is predicated on the principle of causality.

Chapter 10

33. Mantra: A combination of words or more correctly sounds which ,when repeated orally multiple times, is supposed to produce some good or evil effects.

34.Sutra: A series of lines in a Sanskrit text , complete in itself and dealing with a specific story and a connected message/stipulation.

35. Agnitvam: In sacrifices, a huge fire is lighted and goodies like ghee, flowers etc are put into it as offerings to God or any other particular deity of worship. Here, Agni or fire represents the sacred supreme spirit. Only persons possessing the right knowledge and devotion can handle such matters. And this quality on the part of the practitioner is called Agnitvam.

36.Upanayanam: One of the many rites of passage for the higher castes. It is the ceremony marking the wearing of a thread called the sacred thread by a boy and it signifies the boy's second birth to carry out his specific karma.

37.Dakshina: The fees that is paid to the priest for his services .But it is not reckoned as much as fees, as a symbolic offering or gift.

38.Annexure 3: Omitted

9 798887 725284

Printed by Libri Plureos GmbH in Hamburg,
Germany